STOP
WORRYING ABOUT
WHAT OTHERS
THINK ABOUT YOU
AND DISCOVER
WHAT IT IS
GOD SEES
IN YOU

.

INTRODUCTION

As a small business owner I get the pleasure of serving hundreds of businesses. As I make office visits and phone calls I get to know very personal things about these employees and business owners. They share with me their successes and their disappointments.

To an assortment of these businesses I've become their very own cheer squad. When I come into the office they may be down, but when I leave they're pumped up. What I've discovered over the last decade is that many people are living unmotivated, unfilled, depressed, and disappointed lives. Many are stuck in a survival cycle. This became very clear while chatting with my neighbor. I asked a retired neighbor of mine what was it that she always wanted to do? She stared into space then glanced at me and said *"Survival, I've spent my whole life just trying to survive. And I'm still just trying to survive."* It crushed me inside and I felt her pain. My own instinct leans more towards **by any means necessary**. I like to test the waters and swim against the current.

I want to see people being 100% who God made and designed them to be. I want to see people working and functioning in the skills that God gave them. This book is about living the best version of yourself. I know an accountant that is now a bee keeper and she's far happier playing with the bees than the numbers. I have another friend that was a successful financial planner but it was wrecking his health. He quit and a short time later he became a park ranger, he and his wife! This book speaks

BEWARE OF DREAM KILLERS

PART I

A Believers Journey To Getting More Out of Life

ARTEMUS PIERSON

PLP PIERSON LEGACY
PUBLISHING LLC

ELBERT, COLORADO

For general information on other products and services please contact us at: PlegPub@gmail.com

This material contains biblical references.

ISBN [HC] 979-8-9889925-0-9
ISBN [SC] 979-8-9889925-1-6,
ISBN [Epub] 979-8-9889925-2-3
ISBN [SC] BN 979-8-9889925-3-0

Library of Congress Control Number: 2023915720

Hear, O Israel: The Lord our God is one Lord: And thou shalt Love The Lord Thy God wit all thine Heart, with all thy Soul, and With all thy Might. And These Words, Which I command Thee this day, shall be in thine Heart: and thou shalt teach them Diligently unto thy children, and shalt talk of them when thou sittest In thine house, and when thou walkest by the way, & when thou liest down, & when thou risest Up. Duet 6:4-7

TABLE OF CONTENTS

BEWARE OF DREAM KILLERS

Preface   7
Introduction   10
Acknowledgments   13
Change   16
Your Words   22
Accountability   32
Thought Life   43
Just Believe   48
The Nursery Principle   55
The Laser Theory   63
Kingdom   67
Scarcity   71
Power and Authority   80
Producers   90
Identity   103
Receiving   114

MORE STRAY THOUGHTS

The Rich Young Ruler   120
Jesus Was Not Poor   121
Staying Humble   122

THE ART OF STORYTELLING

She Called Me Friend   126
Witches Too?   128
To Grow or Not to Grow   130
100 or 500   131
The Praying Lady   133
Bionic Cowboy   135
Tanks But No Thanks   137
No Eggsplanation Needed   139
Walking In The Dark   142
Weeping Prayer   148
Conclusion   150

PREFACE

Back in the summer of 2017 on my 5a.m. morning walk, I was listening to my bible. I had just completed the portion of Numbers where the Hebrews had sent the spies into the land and the "rulers among them" came back with negative reports.

I was commenting aloud to myself about their cowardly response. *"Aren't these the chosen people, and their leaders go scout the land and come back with this lame report? That's just stupid. Why wouldn't they go possess the land like God already promised them? Why would these people walk around in the desert for forty years when the promise land is right around the corner. Couldn't be me. That don't make no sense!"*

"You've been doing the same thing." It came in a big solid voice, it was internal, yet it felt audible at the same time. I spun around to see if someone was walking behind me. It freaked me out, honestly. I stopped my bible app because the overlapping voice was distracting. *"You've been walking in the wilderness for years. You've done exactly what they did."* {It felt like, *who are you to judge*} It was facetious, practical, but pointy at the same time. I just got check'd by God (or the holy spirit). Then the revelation came. *"My people do what's comfortable. They are afraid of change and would rather do what's familiar. Very few make it to where I want to take them."*

ASTONISHED. SADDENED. CONFUSED. HUMBLED. CORRECTED. BLESSED. STARTLED. HONORED. EXCITED.

After this interaction, my prayers changed dramatically. As our relationship changed my prayers became simpler yet very intentional, not to mention personal. Instead of asking for favors or pleading, I begin asking for guidance. How do I do this, if not this then what? What do I need to do in this situation? I was experiencing information overload. I didn't want him to stop the "sharing" so I prayed and asked him to show me how to manage it all. It was like eating a spiritual onion: potent, tangy, and makes you want to cry. Layer after layer, book after book he kept pouring it on.

There were times when I shared something I read on Tuesday with my wife, and the pastor would mention the same thing on Sunday. I would finish the pastors sentence in his sermon. As I became more familiar with Him these things startled me less.

18 months after quarantine started I was heading to the bank to close on a emergency business loan. Praying in the car, he started "sharing" and I was laughing by the time I arrived at the bank. Just as before, he was straight to the point. He told me *if I actually did the stuff* he was sharing I wouldn't have to ask a prayer like *that* again.

BE ALL THAT GOD CREATED YOU TO BE
DO WHAT IS NECESSARY
HAVE ALL THAT GOD DESIRES FOR YOU

So this book is an act of obedience, me pouring out what God has shared with me and revealed to me because I asked him specific questions. If by the end of this book you don't believe something I encourage you to **ask of him** and **study** to see what he reveals to you.

If anything conflicts with your beliefs, do as my dad would say "Chew on the meat and spit the bones out." It's not my job to persuade you one way or another but to share with you what I've had the privilege to learn. **God Bless.**

a lot about prosperity but know that when I mention prosperity at ANY POINT in this book it is from a point of stewardship. Nothing we have is ours. It all belongs to God; by understanding that you won't get it misconstrued as greed. It's not your home or money, it never was! Every motive and decision should be made from a steward point of view.

The naming of this book, Beware of Dream Killers, was very intentional. Sometimes it can be very hard to see the obvious even when it's right in front of us, and simple. Because it's so simple we think that can't possibly be the solution. God likes to hide truths in plain site to confuse the wise. His ways truly are higher than our ways.

My hope is this book quickens your spirit and allows you to grow and flourish. The concepts and revelations I have received arose from specific questions I asked in prayer. As God through the Holy Spirit revealed things to me, I was guided and directed to books and material that peeked my curiosity and made me rediscover my love for reading. Each book I read would bring me back to the word of God where I would evaluate my understanding of the truth that was revealed to me.

God revealed to me that our dreams and visions are unique to each and every one of us. God only gives us dreams and visions that He knows we can achieve. It is entirely up to us to believe that we can achieve what He has placed in us. The Father will never force our hand unless it's critical to his plan (ex. Jonah, Noah, Jesus). He allows us the opportunity to participate in his plan if we're open and available.

In Beware of Dream Killers I emphasize the urgency of being impeccable with your word, meaning what you say, and standing behind it. Since our words are so important we should be cautious how we use them, they are one of the largest agents of change we have at our disposal.

As I share accountability it's not the typical concept of accountability that we're accustomed to. We are all individually running a race and we are responsible for how we finish the race. As we live our individual lives we should be advocating for each other. Am I my brothers keeper? Yes, I am. Hebrews 3:13, we are called to exhort and uplift one another.

Our individual task is to complete the purpose that is assigned to us. When we depart this life we should all leave empty. Give God everything you have and leave it on the table. By doing this you will be a true steward.

What we believe about God is paramount. What we believe about ourselves is important as well. Our beliefs can limit how He is able to work through us. The one thing that hinders belief is unbelief.

I believe that we can all step into the vision God has given us. As a passionate business owner and believer I regularly advocate and encourage people to discover what it is they were called to do. This book is about self discovery, thanksgiving, and change. May this book draw you closer to our Lord and the person he designed you to be! Go out and be the **UNICORN** He wanted you to be. Be well. Amen.

Throughout the text you will see I.I.W. which is *"It is written"*. This my way of highlighting important scripture and encouraging the retention of scripture. When Jesus spoke he always referenced scripture in this nature. "It is written..." I believe that believers should know scripture as an offensive tool.

I.I.W - Matt 22:36-40

36Master, which is the great commandment in the law? 37Jesus said unto him, Thou shalt love the Lord thy God with all thy heart, and with all thy soul, and with all thy mind. 38This is the first and great commandment. 39And the second is like unto it, Thou shalt love thy neighbour as thyself. 40On these two commandments hang all the law and the prophets.

There are also areas called "Stray Thoughts" that have tidbits of information related to the material in specific chapters. These are just unique side notes that I felt were important enough to share.

ACKNOWLEDGMENTS

I'd like to thank my wife, Kimberly Pierson, for listening to my endless chatter and bearing with me as I figured it all out. Thank you for listening even when you'd already heard everything so many times. Thank you for dreaming with me even when I felt the task was enormous. Thank you for loving the eccentric individual God made me.
Love you dearly, Kimberly.

Many thanks to my friends and family who encouraged and gave me feedback.

(In No Particular Order)
(Mom) Patricia Ingram, (Dad) Nathanael Pierson, Tasha Ramisetti-Gill, Tyrone Smith, Andre Sommerset, Andrea Davis, Nicole Saffon, Simone Severo, and Mark Andre

Abba, Jeshua, and Holy Spirit thank you for every great thing in my life. Without you there truly is no me. Thank you for being a father when mine wasn't available. Thank you for being my counselor when I was too prideful to seek one. Thank you for being a helper when I refused help. Most of all, Thank you for saving me from myself.

God, This will always be about you and me.
Thank You - Thank You - Thank You
Bless you Father!

BEWAR
EOFDR
EAMKI
LLERS

Change

I.I.W. - Joshua 1:9
Have I not commanded thee? Be strong and of a
good courage; be not afraid, neither be thou
dismayed : for the Lord thy God is with thee
wheresoever thou goest.

Never Easy

Change is not easy. Change was never designed to be that way. We're designed to react to change adversely as a survival mechanism. Since our subconscious mind operates on auto pilot it sees change as a threat…until we signal that the change is something we want. As you continue to do the activity that's uncomfortable, the brain adjusts and views the new activity as an acceptable task and makes room in the subconscious for the new activity. The longer you do this activity the easier it gets for the subconscious to set that task on autopilot. This is why people close the door behind themselves after they enter a home. The subconscious is making your life easier by managing this simple task for you. We also know that all the things we do aren't always for our betterment which is why we want to change them.

When we want to change something, all the distress we feel needs to be weighed internally against the change we seek. Treat it like a risk vs reward scenario. Is the reward of losing weight worth the inconvenience of working out and smaller meals? Are the extra hours at work worth the promotion? Is the discomfort and inconvenience of counseling worth the better version of you? Whenever you make dramatic changes, always weigh the change against the reward. If the reward is something you really want then the change is worth the sacrifice. Anything worthwhile will ask you to sacrifice something of yourself.

Opposition

Be prepared to experience push back when you make a significant change in your life. Not only is change big in your life, but also to those around you. When you change; those around you, coworkers and loved ones, will be affected. You're not the only one who doesn't like change. As you assert yourself to meet the goal you want, others may be "inconvenienced". Your routine, behaviors, and temperament are changing and those around you aren't making those same changes. That's not necessarily good or bad, it's just a fact of the matter. Don't expect others to adopt your change for your sake although some may be accommodating. This is your change not theirs.

Do It Anyway

Even if the change you look to make isn't quick, simple, or easy, do it anyway. If it does not harm you or harm another and will help you be a better version of yourself, do it anyway. People tend to stop doing things that are challenging because easy is well, easy! In this current "microwave society" we need it quick, fast, and simple. Strangely, some of the best results come after the hardest work. No matter how hard the new task is, DO IT ANYWAY!

Do Better

We are true creatures of habit. We do what is familiar and we do it often. The brain is wired to do the routine to save as much energy as possible. Which is why you can do a common task then ask moments later if you did that and someone will politely confirm that you did indeed. This subconscious autopilot is great for some things but not all. If you continue doing the same thing, you'll keep getting the same result. If you're reading this you might be tired of the results you've been getting. Well, so was I; and I was tired of watching others win. Don't mistake me, I can appreciate seeing others prosper... it let's me know it's possible! I just want to enjoy prosperity as well. Simple Fact.

Mediocre is not in our makeup. The creator made us to be *magnificent* and *impressive*. Not for you to get the fame and attention but for him to get the glory. Every miracle, every healing, every time

IF YOU KNEW BETTER

YOU WOULD DO BETTER

God has come to the rescue, it has been for his glory. He does not, I repeat, does not share His glory.

I recently learned to show myself some grace. It's more common for us to be gracious and forgiving to others but be pretty harsh on our selves. I say we, meaning me. In counseling I learned a simple principle. We make decisions based off of our history, what we're familiar with, and what we understand at the time.

Simply put, judging the past you on today's knowledge base is harsh. Twenty years ago you didn't have the same level of emotional competence and understanding. The version of you in high school didn't understand that you *really* need to pay attention in class or else. This younger version of you didn't understand that Jane or Jimmy isn't the love of your life and you'll be perfectly fine without them. We make the best decision with the information we have at the moment and trust that the decision will yield the best for us and others. That's it! The indulgent whining and regret games are *horrible mental stimulation*. That "what-if" game is depleting, distracting, and taking your attention away from the present, which is what you do have the ability to change.

IF YOU KNEW BETTER, YOU WOULD DO BETTER

I.I.W. - James 1:8
A double minded man is unstable in all his ways.

Make The Decision, No Wavering

The double mindedness referenced is when your subconscious mind and conscious mind are not in agreement. Your words and conscious mind need to align with the actions the subconscious mind is displaying. The subconscious does only what is stored in its memory or what you've embedded into it. When we witness people doing these contrary things they appear like liars, *or unstable in all their ways.*

WHEN YOU **MAKE A DECISION** AND KNOW WHAT YOU WANT ANYTHING THAT DOES NOT LINE UP WITH THAT DECISION IS NO LONGER AN OPTION.

Brainwashing has such a bad wrap. But the only way to make the subconscious mind and the conscious mind consistent is for you to brainwash yourself. The subconscious is running a program, you just need to alter the program running. The same manner in which we learned the behavior is how we unlearn the same behavior. By repetition you "wash" the mind. After so many cycles of repeating the desired habit or thought the mind will begin creating new memory paths to access these new tasks quicker.

Indecision is debilitating and hinders progress. Your family says they're hungry and your son suggests pizza. You spend 30 minutes sorting through options. After 30 minutes you decide on pizza anyway. You wasted all that time to come up with the same choice that was presented first. This example may just be food but we do this in so many other instances.

Decide what you want, make a decision, and stick with your decision. I know this isn't always so cut and dry, but the sooner you get into the habit of being decisive the easier other decisions will be.

GPS - God's Positioning System

Even if you make a poor decision God is able to correct. Take for instance, when Israel didn't go possess the promise land, and they stayed in the wilderness for 40 years. They still entered the promise land, just later than God had intended. God will always provide a way out but you have to be aware and recognize it. The same happened with Jonah and after three days he was ready to do what was asked of him. God never invades our free will but poor decisions have consequence. You may just have to eat some soggy pizza, stay in a fish for three days, or be stuck in the desert.

SECTION SUMMARY

Never Easy
Change is not easy. Change was never designed to be that way. Weigh all the distress you feel against the change you seek.

Opposition
Be prepared to encounter push back when you make a significant change in your life.

Do It Anyway
No matter how hard the new task is DO IT ANYWAY!

Do Better
If you knew better, you would do better. Make the best decision with the information you have at the moment and trust that the decision will yield the best outcome for you and others.

Make The Decision, No Wavering
Make a decision and stick with your decision. Indecision is debilitating and hinders progress.

GPS - God's Positioning System
Even when you make a poor decision God is able to correct. God always provides a way out but you have to recognize it.

What is it you'd like to change in your life?
Who benefits from this change if you initiate it?
How long will it take you to change this?
What about this change are you fearful of?

Your Words
Gifts of Creation

I.I.W. - Proverbs 6:2
Thou art ensnared by the words of thy mouth,
thou art taken with the words of thy mouth.

Mankind takes the power of the spoken word for granted. We spend our childhood years learning how to write and assemble words into sentences so we can best share what we're feeling and communicate our thoughts. But are we aware that our words have power? We may be aware of some of their power but not to the level they truly contain.

Creation Power

Our words hold the power to create or destroy. We can build people up or tear them down with one sentence. Words were given to use as a creation tool. Oftentimes they are misused. Eloquent speakers understand this and use them as such. Dictators, politicians, and clergy fully understand this and wield them accordingly.

In Gen 1:3 God said, "let there be light: and there was light." And God said, and God said, and God said…(again and again) and God saw everything that he had made, and behold, it was very good. Who is God saying these things to? At this moment there is only Him (The Godhead) and endless energy. The law of spoken word is being demonstrated from the very beginning! Though our naked eyes may not perceive and see the limitless energy between us and other objects next to us, it does not mean those elements do not exist.

Our Words Are Energy

Have you ever been in a heated argument and noticed you're exhausted afterward? You may not have exerted any physical energy but you are immediately tired because of it. Words carry energy and command energy. Football coaches understand this. Players drag their feet into the locker room after a horrendous first half and after an exhilarating speech the team emerges the second half and wipes the other team out. If you could be a fly on the wall and see one man surrounded by a bunch of gladiators hopping up and down leaning into his every word. *That's* what words do when they're used correctly, they bring things to life. Use them wisely.

Watch What You Say

The blatant misuse of words is obvious in some cultures. How often have you heard someone say "I think I'm getting sick, That's to die for, You're killing me, You make me sick, You're always in trouble, You're not that smart, You're dumb". You get the point. Telling your friends and loved one harmful things have long term damage, especially if they believe you. After all, why wouldn't they believe you? You're the ones closest to them. We are to speak life into each others life. Only God knows the potential buried inside of each one of us. It's our job to nurture one another so the world can see our fruit. We will be remembered by the fruit we bear. (Luke 6:44)

Bishop Milton Wright had two sons, Wilbur and Orville, who shared with him their vision of flight. He responded by calling it "Heresy, flight is reserved for the angels." He responded. "If God had intended for man to fly, he would have given him wings." The bishop then took it a step further and ministered a message in front of his congregation about it. The sons pressed on with a defiant spirit proving their father wrong. The Wright brothers willingness to stick with their dream gifted mankind with air travel. Well, one Wright was wrong. Two Wrights were right! The rest you can say is history.

Negative words empower and place negative things into action. When you speak negative words you are inviting those things to take place. Nothing happens without a prompt! All things are initiated with words, which is why you should not speak those things into existence. You have the power to nullify negativity by speaking positively.

Speak What You Seek Until You See What you Spoke

One word spoken into your life has the ability to carry you through all your life. Make a concerted effort to speak hope, love, and life over each other. You could be the inspiration someone has been waiting for, bringing the word they've needed to hear their whole life. You may be the light cutting through the darkness in their life.

Speak What You Want Done

There is "energy" waiting for you to put it into action. When we abdicate our role as the co-creator *we allow* things to "just happen". We were given full dominion, authority and power over everything on this earth. None of the desirable results we look for will come without our permission. What we permit is what we will see. (see also Kingdom, Power and Authority)

I.I.W. - Matt 18:18

Verily I say unto you, Whatsoever ye shall bind on earth shall be bound in heaven: and whatsoever ye shall loose on earth shall be loosed in heaven.

Jesus *said* to the fig tree "no man will eat hereafter ever" (after this). I know he's Jesus the messiah, but Jesus is showing the disciples the power of words. I'm very confident that he could have laid hands on the tree and it would've grown fruit instantly. As they returned the same direction the next morning Peter reminded him of the tree he spoke to the previous day. Jesus immediately goes into "whosoever shall say unto this mountain"..once again reiterating SAY WHAT YOU WANT and believe. Say what you want, say what you want, say what you want. And ONLY say what you want! Quit speaking things that you don't want to happen. The sooner we unlearn that poor habit the better off we'll all be.

Speak what you seek until you see what you spoke. Though brief and simple, the notion is profoundly powerful. If you did that you would be invoking the power of the spoken word, initiating faith, putting faith into action, and embracing hope in wait of its result or manifestation. Faith is the currency that the kingdom utilizes. The longer you speak things the more you believe them. When we believe, then it can be produced in the physical. Cultivators create the conditions they seek to plant the desires they look to achieve.

Written Word

Why should we write things down? There is undeniable power in the written word. Christians have even coined the term, "The Word," when referring to the bible. Since the beginning of time long before paper and papyrus were being used we scratched in the sand and scribbled on walls and tablets. The desire to share and make our thoughts known to others has always been present.

For over five millennia certain segments of society were not allowed to read or write. They were treated as beasts of burden. The elitist wanted them to work, not to be distracted with reading and writing. Writing manages to engage your mind and allow you to look at things from another angle. The last thing they wanted was the working class planning a way out of servitude and inspiring each other. Thus, knowing how to write was frowned upon and even punishable. The empowered individuals understood the need for literacy and the power the written word evoked.

Throughout history, conquering armies often destroyed the library where books, collections of history, and inspiration were housed. Destroying the libraries sent a signal to the occupants that they were under new rule. Reigning rulers understood that the written word would give an occupied territory a degree of hope and hope would lead to uprising and dissension. The spoken word can be fleeting, but the written word has the ability to be permanent, written on our hearts and minds. We have many ways we learn. These are four of the core styles.

VISUAL • AUDITORY • READING + WRITING • KINESTHETIC

Writing is so important, which is why it's one of the first skills instilled in us at an early age. It's a life skill. With all the advancements in technology it's sad that writing has become so insignificant to so many people. The written word has been substituted by digital word which can be erased with ease. Writing brings clarity to our ideas and thoughts. Writing is one of the many things that differentiates us from the rest of God's creations. We are his greatest creation!

Power of the Pen

When you write something down you are in essence making it "official". Yes, we make verbal agreements, but a written agreement is harder to contest. In Britain they abolished slavery with the stroke of a

The Pen is Mightier Than The Sword

pen, whereas America tried to abolish slavery forcibly and were thrust into civil war for 4 years with greater than 620,000 casualties. This number is the largest number of casualties at that time America had ever seen in a single conflict. In the third year of the war the Emancipation Proclamation was passed. Once again showing the pen truly is mightier than the sword.

Writing Goals

Why do speakers, teachers, and planners make you write your goals? There really is a reason behind it. It's not just to keep you busy. Writing down goals has a biological response. Your mind will encode the information and store it in memory. Things you write will hold higher importance in your mind than the things you've heard. This encoding helps your subconscious mind recall better what it is you're trying to accomplish. The act of writing it down adds a visual effect so that you can reference it later whenever you look at it. So writing the goals has a compound effect. (Forbes 2018)

I.I.W. - Habakkuk 2:2
Write the vision, and make it plain upon tablets,
that he may run that readeth.

Before most financial planners begin assisting you they have you write down your financial goals. Once you've written down your goals they can proceed to help you. It's not real until you write them down. Up to that point your goals were just a lofty idea. Writing them down instantly makes you accountable to yourself. Now you have to measure up to what you said you wanted. Writing your goals down makes you accountable. People are *easy forgetters*, we have fleeting thoughts from moment to moment. Take for instance if you've ever journaled and you come across your own writing at a later time. Some of the things you wrote earlier may seem new to you if it's been a lengthy amount of time since you wrote them. While you're in that moment you're instantly whisked away to that moment in time when you originally wrote those thoughts down. Writing has that beautiful effect! Just write it down. You won't be sorry.

When writing your goals make them in the present tense. Make them personal, use *I*, and make them positive. (ex. I am in the top 10% of sales this year, I have lost 30 lbs., I run 2 miles a day, etc.) Do not use ***don't*** or ***not*** in any of your phrasing. *Your subconscious mind likes to actually do everything that precedes the {no, don't, can't}.* Keep all your goal setting on the positive side. You can be specific and set timed or dated goals. I don't always set a date. I like to allow some room for God to work things out. He hasn't failed me yet.

SECTION SUMMARY
Creation Power
We can build people up or tear them down with one sentence. Our words hold the power to create or destroy.

Our Words Are Energy
Words carry energy and command energy.

Watch What You Say
Make a concentrated effort to speak hope, love, and life to each other. It's our job to nurture one another.

Speak What You Want Done
There is energy waiting for you to put it into action. What we permit is what we will see.

Written Word, Power of the Pen
Writing engages your mind and allows you to look at a different angle. When you write things down you are in essence making them official.

Writing Goals
Writing goals has a biological response. The things you write, your mind will hold higher importance to, than the things you've heard.

STRAY THOUGHTS. CHEW ON THIS..

The rice & water test by Dr. Masaru Emoto

Three beakers or jars are equally filled with rice and water. Each day for thirty days Jar 1 is spoken to positively, Jar 2 is spoken to negatively, and Jar 3 is ignored.

At 30 days Jar 1, the positive jar was fermenting but showed no signs of mold. Jar 2, the negative jar had a considerable amount of mold growth. Jar 3, the ignored jar had more mold than the negative jar.

Dr. Emoto then took water samples and froze them to look at crystal formations underneath a microscope. The positive water sample had intricate beautiful crystal formations. The negative and ignored water sample had deformed unnatural formations. The experiment closes with the noted assumption that water carries energy, emotions, and remembers.

My Observation

If water can transmit energy and remember, what does that mean for humans? If humans are made of more than 60% water, and our blood is 90% water...what kind of negative/positive energy are we carrying around? How much negative/positive reinforcement have we been subjected to? The worst part is that the neglected sample was in worse condition than the negative sample each time. Therefore meaning it's just as bad to neglect something as it is to berate it.

Have you used your words to help or harm?
Do you uplift your fellow man/woman?
Are you encouraging or discouraging?
Do you set goals? Do you write them down?
Do you keep up with your goal achievement?
What does it feel like when you accomplish a goal?
What learning style do you identify with?

If you could have your dream job/career what are the most important qualities that would need to be present?

1. List 10-15 key qualities important to you.
Ex. freedom of schedule, financial independence, freedom to share faith openly, great team, cohesive team, traveling, work with family, community impact

2. Narrow down your list. See what the four most important qualities are by comparing them.
Ex. Great team vs. community impact:
Great Team
Ex. Work with family vs freedom of schedule:
Freedom of schedule

This exercise will help you identify what's important to you at your core. There are no wrong answers because these are what's important to you.
After you've identified your three or four main qualities, ask God in prayer how to get to that point.

Accountability
Who's To Blame

I.I.W. - Jere 31:33-35
but this shall be the covenant that I will make with the
house of Israel; After those days, saith the LORD, I will put
my law in their inward parts, and write it in their hearts; and
will be their God, and they shall be my people.

Accountability is one of those things most people would rather not talk about. I'm not going to harp on how you should be accountable to your family, your friends, or coworkers. We're not going to grumble about how you should own your mistakes and deal with the repercussions. Those things are already a given, we all know we should own our mistakes. Wasting precious time on that is useless; besides that's a whole 'nother book all together.

The Kingdom of heaven doesn't allow us the privilege of shirking our responsibilities. As Kingdom citizens we are held to a higher standard and accountable to the King and our fellow citizens. We are commanded to love the Lord with all our heart, and our neighbors as ourselves. God gives us direction and guidance so that we would be "set apart", consecrated. This consecration gives us distinction. If we look, live, and function just as everyone else there is no distinction. *"But you are a chosen generation, a royal priesthood, an holy nation, a peculiar people;"(1 Peter 2:9a)* We should be different than the rest of society!

Not Your Shame & Guilt

When dealing with accountability we have to address feelings that are uncomfortable. I am not opposed to confronting these feelings but I want you to know personally that God is NOT the origin of those! God is a GOOD FATHER, and The Father corrects, he does not shame. (Heb 12:6, Pro 3:12, Deut 8:5)

Let's make one thing clear. Shame and guilt are not from God. When Isaiah prophesied of the messiah he shared *"Fear not; for thou shalt not be ashamed: neither be confounded; for thou shalt not be put to shame: for thou shalt forget the shame of thy youth, and shalt not remember the reproach of thy widowhood any more. For thy Maker is thine husband; The Lord of hosts is his name; and thy Redeemer the Holy One of Israel; The God of the whole earth shall he be called" (Isa 54: 4,5)*. So, Isaiah foretold of the Christ, then the Christ came and accomplished all that was foretold, and then he ascended. Then Paul reminds us *(Rom 10:11-12)* *"For the scripture saith, Whosoever believeth on him shall not be ashamed. For there is no difference between the Jew and the Greek: for the same Lord over all is rich unto all that call upon him. For whosoever shall call upon the name of the Lord shall be saved."*

Leave Empty

We should all hope that when we leave this life, we leave empty. My personal venture is that I do all I can do, seen all I can see, and act on what God the Father has purposed me to accomplish. That hasn't always been the case though. I've spent a portion of my life just trying to get by and doing whatever I pleased. When I was in one of the darkest moments of my life I cried out to God and he answered, and I made an agreement to follow him and do whatever he needed of me.

> "The richest place on earth is the graveyard, because it is there that you will find all hopes and dreams that were never fulfilled, the books that were never written, the songs that were never sung, the inventions that were never shared, the cures that were never discovered. All because someone was too afraid to take the first step, keep with the problem, or afraid to carry out their dream."
> - Dr. Myles Munroe & Les Brown

That's a tough pill to swallow. It's my understanding that we don't get a "do-over" in the end. That disturbs me. We need to empty the tank, go to the grave empty. Pour out all you have to give while you can; to help and enrich the lives of those who you can help. There is an event or person waiting for you to be obedient to what God has instilled and enlisted you to do. Will you do it? Can you see it? Do you even know?

I spend a lot of time with people older than myself. A large portion of my circle of friends are retired people aged 50 to 75. I benefit greatly from these friends because they speak from experience and not speculation. They have seen and outlived things I couldn't imagine. At a young age I gravitated to the elders in the community. My great grandmother would share with me the oddest things, things she didn't share with my aunts and uncles. I relished when we were alone, because if she was in the mood she'd share what it was like growing up in the early 1900's. Oh man, Madear, my great grandmother could paint a picture. That made sense since she was born in a generation that predated TV. Without the use of pictures or television you need to be very detailed to get a point across. She did a fine job of that!

One of my greatest concerns in our American culture is the lack of engagement with the older generation. The whole retirement idea sort of disturbs me. I see so many older Americans left alone just short of abandonment. **Everyone brings something to the table.** The early 1900's experienced so many challenges that this generation could learn from. There's a wealth of knowledge and experience just sitting cooped up in their homes. These people could be help in society as mentors and friends. Remember, the goal is to leave here empty!

I.I.W. - Pro 3:27
Do not withhold good from those to whom
it is due,when it is in your power to act.

In this chapter I'm hoping to ignite the *willingness* to engage with God and see, if not do, what it is he has for you to do. As you complete this book "The Art of Storytelling" is at the end. There I've shared some personal stories about myself and things I've seen God do with me and others. His ways are truly above our ways (Isa 55:8-9). Don't get me wrong, it's not always comfortable but it's always rewarding to see how he works.

YESTERDAY IS HISTORY,
TOMORROW IS A MYSTERY,
TODAY IS A GIFT OF GOD,
THAT'S WHY IT'S CALLED
THE PRESENT.
- BIL KEANE -

For God shall bring every work into judgment, with every secret thing. Whether it be good, or whether it be evil.

Unforgiveness

What if forgiveness was just an idea? NO, forgiveness is required.

Unforgiveness is extremely toxic and a blessing blocker. Unforgiveness leaves the tortured one sick. I say tortured because the large majority of the time the offender has gone on with their life and continued living and others are left "holding the bag". This shouldn't be the case. You're angry, frustrated and upset, and they're doing whatever they do, and not angry. That's why the acts of forgiveness and repentance are basic tasks that are part of our core values as believers. **Confessing** your sins (One to another). **Repentance** of transgressions. Ask for <u>forgiveness</u>. *"If we confess our sins, he is faithful and just to forgive us our sins, and to cleanse us from all unrighteousness" 1 John 1:9.*

Maybe forgiveness is just a suggestion? NO, forgiveness is required.

When we harbour unforgiveness it limits how the kingdom can function and work with us. *"if my people, which are called by my name, shall humble themselves, and pray, and seek my face, and turn from their wicked ways; then will I hear from heaven, and will forgive their sin, and will heal their land" 2 Chr 7:14.*

This is why Jesus spoke of forgiveness so much. We need access to heaven all the time. We don't want to cut ourselves off from being able to communicate with the Father or the Kingdom. Peter asked Jesus, *"How many times can my brother sin against me? Up to seven times?"* Jesus answers, *"I say not seven times, but seventy times seven" Matt 18:21-22.* Then Jesus illustrates the act of forgiveness and judgment in parable, of course!

Roughly paraphrased: *"Therefore the Kingdom of heaven is like a king that wanted to settle his accounts with his servants. One servant was brought to him that owed ten thousand talents (tremendous sum). The servant was unable to pay and he and his family were ordered to be sold. The servant fell at his feet and pleaded not to be sold. "Master have patience with me, I will pay you everything." The Master was moved with compassion, released him, and forgave the debt. The same servant then went and found another servant that owed him a small fraction of what he owed (measly sum). He grabbed the other servant by the throat and demanded he pay what he owe. Other servants were grieved and went and told the*

Master what the servant had done. The Master was furious after hearing this. "You wicked servant, I forgave you all the debt because you begged me. Shouldn't you have compassion on your fellow servant just as I had pity on you?" His Master was angry and sent him to the tormentors until he should pay all his debt. "So My heavenly Father also will do to you if each of you, from his heart, does not forgive his brother his trespasses." Matt 18:35

Wow, do I need to mention the numerous mentions of money in this parable! Jesus has NO issue whatsoever bringing money into the conversation. Money appears in many of his parables. Debts, trespasses, offenses, and sin against each other appear to be equally wrong in the Kingdom of heaven. Food for thought.

In the Lord's Prayer when he was giving guidance on how to pray, forgiveness was included. *"Forgive us our debts, as we forgive our debtors" Matt 6:12.* Then after the prayer he states again. *"For if you forgive men their trespasses, your heavenly Father will also forgive you: but if you forgive not men their trespasses, neither will your Father forgive your trespasses" Matt 14:15.*

EXERCISE IN FORGIVENESS - TRY THIS

In your prayer time ask is there anyone you need to forgive or anyone you need to make amends with. You might be surprised how many people come to mind.

Jesus also took care to mention that in the process of giving offering that we should reconcile with our brother/sister prior to giving the offering. *²³Therefore if thou bring thy gift to the altar, and there rememberest that thy brother hath ought against thee; ²⁴leave there thy gift before the altar, and go thy way; first be reconciled to thy brother, and then come and offer thy gift" Matt 5:23-24.*

We should strive to stay in a constant posture to forgive. The power, spirit, and energy forgiveness releases to you is monumental. I'm not suggesting we be weak or gullible, but meek and pliable. We live in an dynamic world, everything changes all the time. We need to be rooted but learn to sway when the wind pushes.

Values

Character is defined by your value system. Our mental and moral qualities define our character. Our character traits are how someone would describe us if they were describing us to another individual. When someone mentions you how would they describe you apart from your physical attributes? Are you compassionate, are you surly? Would they consider you quiet or a social butterfly like myself? Are you driven and disciplined? I try to treat life as if I were writing a eulogy. How I live my life now is how I want to be remembered. What will they say about you?

If I'm being honest my value system hasn't always been upright. Today *honesty, resourcefulness,* and *loyalty* are my most important values. My family and friends would agree that I have a broken filter. I usually say what's on my mind and apologize if I feel I offended anyone. The key there is *when I feel I've offended*, you see how that could be problematic. I admit that I've progressed over the years and become more tactful. But today, right now, what you see is what you get. Because of these two values, honesty and loyalty, my family doesn't have to worry about me hiding things from them or sneaking around. They also know they can come to me with certain things and I'll be available. Because I value resourcefulness I make it a point to be of value and help when possible in my business and personal life. These three values are also identified by others outside of my inner circle.

People feel compelled to tell me the oddest things. I Identified this when I first got saved in prison. Prior to my release I considered becoming a CDC (Chemical Dependency Counselor) but I decided against it because I didn't want the daily burden. So for two decades I've been an interned unpaid sounding board for peoples personal problems. God truly has a strange sense of humor. A friend of mine once called me a paraclete (parakletos). I had to research what that even meant, para [come alongside] + kalein [called], one called to come alongside, an advocate. So a paraclete is one who comes alongside his brother/sister similar to a counselor in court.

My character and value system are what drive me; even in my occupations. I've always made employment decisions based on if I would be helpful and what are they paying. As I've aged the ability to be helpful has been more important. My clients know that if I can help, that I will. To me that's important. To you that may not be the driving force, but for me impact and resourcefulness are key. This is exactly why this book was produced. The need for me to help people and be obedient to God is my motivation. If I can save you a few gray hairs and headaches I'm all for it.

Judgment

One of the most difficult habits I've noticed believers struggle and stumble with is judgment. We masks our judgments with complicated terms to justify making these judgments. So let me just lay out all the terms so we can be clear: biases, prejudices, speculations, stereotypes, and even assumptions. When you enter a room full of people you need to be able to determine if it's a safe space. I wholeheartedly understand that some judgments are survival skills that are involuntary and learned. My question is, when are we judging too much?

"Judge not, that ye be not judged. ²For with what judgment ye judge, ye shall be judged: and with what measure ye mete, it shall be measured to you again." (Matt 7:1-2)

Two decades ago, I wasn't a believer and was comfortable sinning. I am the cumulative result of dozens of people praying for me. If you met me back then you wouldn't recognize me. It's amazing how people can change! See that's the problem with judgment, we never really know God is working. Also, placing judgment is exalting our opinion over God's. People could have easily assumed I'd never change or that I was a lost cause. Given the facts they would have been correct in thinking that. *But God.* But God in his infinite wisdom knows our beginning and our end. God works on all of us in his own distinctive manner. We want instant results but God's plans have to unravel. God makes a way where there is no way. We live with facts but God works on faith. The people who prayed for me had faith that God would intervene in my life. We each have a purpose but we have to grow and develop. The challenges we face can strengthen us if we allow them to.

Matthew 7:2 states that what measure you meet, it will be measured to you. How would you like to be measured and weighed in the middle. When you're tested you don't get graded until the completion of the test. When someone is in surgery they don't let you come in and evaluate the effectiveness of the surgery in the middle of the process. No, you have to wait until the surgeon puts everything back in place and cleans up after the surgery. A day of judgment is appointed to us all. You can't live your life and mine, just yours. We have the privilege of assisting and coming alongside one another (paraclete). Help each other but do not judge one another on an incomplete work.

Temptation

To temper something is to test it. Which is why temptation is the testing of your character. All of us have different things that we are working on. If you know of your friend's vice, it's your personal responsibility not to lead them into temptation just because it's not a problem for you. Stop asking your friends that struggle with alcohol to happy hour. Stop persuading your friend that's struggles with infidelity to the night club. Stop teasing the friend eating vegetables that has a heart condition and high cholesterol. If you have friends like this encourage them to stop chiding you. If that doesn't deter the "just playing" you may need to evaluate your relationship. We are to be allies and helpmates. When Jesus went to pray he asked the other disciples to *"Pray that you don't fall into temptation." (Luke 22:40)* and they fell asleep and he reminded them to *"Get up and pray so that you will not fall into temptation." (Luke22:46)* I know we aren't being martyred at the moment but the forces of darkness are always acting against the Kingdom of Heaven. Consider, we are intended to come alongside (paraclete), not come against (contend). Iron sharpens iron (Pro 27:17)

When Jesus instructed the disciples on how to pray (Luke 11:4) He closes with *"Forgive us our sins, for we also forgive every one that is indebted to us. And lead us not into temptation; but deliver us from evil."* That last line stumped me at first and lead us not into temptation. Why would I need to ask God not to lead me into temptation. Then, good ol' Job came to mind. God allows us to walk things out before he intercedes, and the Lord will allow us to be tested. So asking him to not lead us into temptation would be like. "Hey, Father if you want to send temptation over this way, I'd like to get a pass on that if you don't mind."

I.I.W. - Jam 1:2-4

²My brethren, count it all joy when ye fall into divers temptations; ³knowing this, that the trying of your faith worketh patience. ⁴But let patience have her perfect work, that ye may be perfect and entire, wanting nothing.

SECTION SUMMARY

Not Your Shame & Guilt
Shame and guilt are not from God.
God is a Good Father, He corrects, He doesn't shame.

Leave Empty
Empty the tank, go to the grave empty.
Everyone brings something to the table.

Unforgiveness
Forgiveness is required, not a suggestion.
Unforgiveness is toxic and a blessing blocker.
Strive to stay in a posture to easily forgive.
The power and energy of forgiveness is monumental.

Values
Our mental and moral qualities define our values.
Be a helper, not a hindrance.

Judgment
Don't judge the results prior to completion of the test.
You placing judgment is placing your opinion over God's.
Help one another, do not judge one another.

Temptation
Temptation is the testing of your character.
We are intended to come alongside, not come against.
The Lord will allow you to be tested.

What guilt or shame are you holding onto?
What's keeping you from letting it go?
Do you believe God forgives everything?
Do you have an issue with unforgiveness?
What values are most important to you?
What are your favorite character traits?
Are you your friend's advocate or an enabler?
Do you have an accountability partner?
Do you have a prayer partner? Prayer community?
Will you be empty when you finish this life?

List 10 things you wish you would have done by now
Ex. Skydiving, written a book, learn to paint

Again, there are no wrong answers.
These are your answers.

Thought Life
Thoughts Create Results

I.I.W. - Phil 4:8

Whatsoever things are true, whatsoever things are honest, whatsoever things are just, whatsoever things are pure, ...lovely,...good report; if there be <u>any</u> virtue, and if there be any praise, THINK on these things.

It is IMPOSSIBLE for you to NOT THINK. Even in our slumber our subconscious is resolving things we have worked on in our waking hours. This happens sort of like defragging a computer, cleaning up the hard drive. The mind being the super computer it is, only wants to execute and deliver what is being input and calculated. Computer programmers know this principle as garbage in, garbage out.

Even at the lowest assumption of 4 thoughts a minute, that's 240 thoughts an hour, 5,760 thoughts a day. So we can't control how many thoughts come to us, but we can decide how we'll react and engage with those thoughts. Even if we take a break from critical thinking we begin taking direction and feeding off of media around us. Not paying attention to what we mentally intake & digest can be detrimental to our overall mental and spiritual health.

Thought Comes First

Nothing comes to manifestation without first being a thought. Thoughts are the seeds of things. Whatever circumstances you're living in are the direct result of the thoughts you have been feeding it. On the same note, you can change your circumstances by meditating on the outcome you seek. Thoughts birth words, words initiate actions, actions create manifestation. *"Guard your heart above all else, for it determines the course of your life."* Pro 4:23 NLT

THOUGHTS ➜ WORDS ➜ ACTIONS ➜ MANIFESTATION

Meditation - Think About It

Meditation tends to be thought of as an eastern concept (yogi, lama, monk, and etc.) But the word meditation denotes deep concentrated thought. Some choose to meditate in silence, while others may recite scripture, a mantra, or affirmations. Verbal meditation works because it allows you to focus and engages the subconscious mind. *"May the words of my mouth and the meditation of my heart be pleasing to you, O Lord, my rock and redeemer."* Psalm 19:14 NLT

If a problem arises you can choose to let it unravel you or hand it over to God. But even then some people still seem bothered. Believers say things like "Give it to God". If you've truly given it to God, you can not continue dwelling on it and running all these scenarios in your head. That continual "thinking" is you meditating on it. Remember, it is impossible for us not to think but we do have control over how we react and engage those thoughts.

Instead, think of ONLY what you seek. Think about the virtuous helpful outcome you desire. The act of worrying is the opposite of faith. Fear is faith in reverse.

We Are Co-Creators

Co-creation is no small feat. We've patterned ourselves to have unhealthy thoughts, speak destructive things and be upset when we have undesired results. Even when we are the cause of a large portion of these results.

I.I.W. - GEN 1:26

And God said, Let **us** make man in **our** image, after **our** likeness: and let them have dominion over the fish, and over the fowl of the air, and over the cattle, over all the earth, and over every creeping thing that creepeth upon the earth.

God buried your future inside you so no one Could Steal it from You!

We are **wonderfully** and **beautifully** made in the image of the Creator. We are purposed to create and lead. Our imagination is the tool that He equipped us with. The two words *Image* and *formation* are where we get the word Imagination. This tool of imagination is powered by your spirit.

As children we exercise our imagination. As we get older our imagination gets dulled and conformity sets in. The weight of responsibility becomes very real. The idea of one day becoming a doctor, astronaut, or president just turns into a fantasy. We see a set pattern that our peers follow and we abandon our dreams. Some dreams that persist and linger in our heart and minds were placed there by the Creator. So do you just continue being "normal" or do you see what it is God intended for you to pursue? The Spirit speaks to our spirit. (Romans 8:16) He planted the seed so it has to be a part of a greater purpose.

I.I.W. - Job 22:28
Though shalt decree a thing, and it shall be established unto thee: and the light shall shine upon thy ways.

The world will always present opportunities for us to speak contrary to the things we desire in our life, for ourselves, and for our family. It is up to us to recognize these opportunities and turn the would-be curses into blessings. God intended for us to be victors, not victims. God endorses freewill, he wants us to make decisions. As strange as that may seem, why else then would a perfect God create fallible beings other than to commune with us and allow us to participate in creation. I'm a firm believer that we are all spiritual beings having an earthly experience. When we depart this life the spirit continues on. Depending on what you believe, some of us will join the Father at that point. I see earth as a big sandbox that the Father wanted to give us the opportunity to play in before we join him for eternity. *(This is my personal opinion, agree or disagree).*

SECTION SUMMARY

Thought Comes First

Nothing comes to manifestation without first being a thought.
Thoughts ➡ Words ➡ Actions ➡ Manifestation
Thoughts are the seeds of things.

Meditation - Think About It

Think ONLY of what you seek. Keep your mind on things that are pure, lovely, good, honest and just. (Phil 4:8)

We Are Co-Creators

We are made in the image of the Creator. Our imagination is the tool we deploy to assist creation. Seek what it is God intended for you to pursue.

Do you have time alone with your thoughts?
Do you have time alone with God?
What do you find yourself thinking about the most?
Do you worry about things you've given to God?

Start a journal, if you haven't already.

Write what you're really thinking & feeling so you can reflect on it later. The best way to learn about yourself is to be honest with yourself.

Just Believe
This is Your Job

What Stopped The Master

This man is in the company of Jesus, the one person known to manifest results. The father is crying out to get help for his son that has "violent fits", throwing him on the ground, in the water, into the fire, and foaming at the mouth. He's told to just believe and his response is "I do, but help my unbelief" (Mark 9). This man is honest enough to openly admit that there is some area of unbelief, so help me with that. In Jesus' own country *"he did not many works because of their unbelief." Matt 13:58*

I.I.W. - Mark 6:6

He marveled because of their unbelief.

For Jesus to be astonished there had to be plenty of unbelief, tons of doubt. There may be an innumerable reasons why someone may be in disbelief. The pivotal moment comes when we can take charge of the moment and place our belief in front of the hard facts. Facts are facts, but belief will trump facts with the right individual and beliefs. Jesus once implied *"Fear not, believe only, and she shall be made whole"*, then moments later he literally brings a deceased girl back to life. (Luke 8:50)

Act As If

Act as if what you dream for is already present. This isn't about faking it till you make it but instead actually seeing it in your mind. Acting is so powerful that actors sometimes get "lost-in-the-role" when they immerse themselves in their character roles. Some of us are acting out tragic stories right now. The roles we're actively engaged in right now are not the roles we want. This is in fact method acting, then all we need to do is switch roles. We can eliminate the stress, insomnia, and depression roles we've adopted. That would make it seem that life in fact is stranger than fiction.

The Placebo Effect:
Patients that are administered a placebo get healing as a result of their belief in the effectiveness of the "drug" they were given; even though the substance was never a real drug capable of remedying the problem.

Imagination

What a beautiful thing! The imagination has endless possibilities but for some unknown reason as we mature we quit using it the way we employed it as a child. As a child, some of us believed we could do anything and go anywhere we dreamed. At least we thought so. Though this may not be true for all children, the sentiment is pure and untainted. As we age people stop believing in the impossible. Some people don't even believe in the possible. But people are continuously doing the impossible everyday. So pretty soon we'll need to use another word for impossible. Improbable or unlikely might be a better fit.

Waiting For Expression

Someone is waiting on you to do what God put in you and they won't be able to complete their journey in the same manner until you begin yours. A relay team can't finish the race until the first and second leg have started running; this is a race and we're in it together.

What is it that calls to you day and night and you can't stop thinking of? What is it that you talk about doing all the time? What dreams lie dormant in your spirit waiting to be expressed, waiting for you to give them life? Will you listen to the dream? Will you nurture and feed the vision?

DON'T BE AFRAID OF BEING **DIFFERENT**.
BE AFRAID OF BEING LIKE EVERYONE ELSE.

I.I.W. - Matt 19:26b
With men this is impossible;
but with God all things are possible.

The list of people who have accomplished the "impossible" is pretty extensive. The common element they all possess and use is their creativity and imagination. When these people start to believe in conquering the impossible they get miraculous results. A few of these individuals were accomplished in more than one occupation - real renaissance men.

Wright Bros., Da Vinci, Columbus, George W. Carver, Ben Franklin, Fredrick Douglas, Usain Bolt, Thomas Edison, Henry Ford, Nikola Tesla, Eli Whitney, Rudolf Diesel, Madam C.J. Walker, Albert Einstein, Louis Pasteur, Louis Braille, Cai Lun (paper), Alexander G. Bell, Thomas Jennings, Robert Fulton (steam engine), Lumière Bros.(movies), and Guglielmo Marconi

Thanks to these *visionaries* we get to enjoy the impossible being commonplace. What is it you'd like to see happen that you once thought impossible?

Visualization

Visualization, is the ability to engage the imagination and mentally see what one desires to attain or achieve. So how does one visualize? That's simple and difficult at the same time. For example, when you apply for a job you *imagine* yourself showing up to work in that position and going through the normal course of the day. You see yourself getting the raise, showing up to the new office, shaking hands with new people. That right there is an example of visualization. The other step would be when you can *feel what it feels like* to be in that position. The joy and excitement you have when you're there in your mind.

Professional athletes see themselves making the touchdown, crossing the finish line, or hitting the home run before they even hit the field. General Contractors can see what a finished project looks like and how it's going to be used while the lot is still a pile of dirt. Lawyers see themselves winning the case and presenting the closing argument. I've heard it said *"Feeling gets the fulfillment"*.

You Are a Receiving Station

I initiated a media purge for myself back in 2021. No news at all. When friends and family start talking about the bad news, I share with them that I don't watch it. My neighbor claims, She wish she could, but she just can't stop watching it. "I hate watching it, it makes me feel so sad". That's the reason you want to stop watching it!

We are a receiving station. We intake information and suggestions willing or unwillingly, our mind being the super computer it is does not care. Our mind works with whatever suggestion is presented to it with the least resistance. Our familiarity with something drops our walls. For example, once an individual sees a company's branding enough times it makes them familiar and more likely to engage with the business, these are called impressions. When the time to use their service arrives you don't hesitate, your familiarity has let your guard down. This simple fact is why businesses spend so much on marketing. It increases their chances of being utilized by your family. Like that plush toy your child has. They couldn't live without, but no longer play with it!

Music has the same suggestive nature. Music improves verbal memory encoding, which is why people know the jingle and song to so many of their favorite brands. This practice of encoding memory was initiated at an early age. Remember when your parents would sing to you as a child. It didn't matter how bad the singing was they were comforting you to sleep. Then, later you learned your nursery rhymes, letters, and numbers the same way. As you continued to progress in grade school you may have employed similar tricks to remember other important tidbits. Marketing teams have spent billions over decades perfecting this art.

Are your beliefs your own? Have we been programmed? How would you change the program if you wanted to?

SECTION SUMMARY
What Stopped the Master
Unbelief was the one thing that hindered Jesus. The pivotal moment comes when we place our belief in front of facts.

Act As If
Act as if what you dream for is already present. Don't fake it till you make it but see it in your mind.

Imagination
To a child the world has endless possibilities. Start dreaming like a child. The imagination has endless possibilities.

Visualization
The formation of a mental image. Feeling gets the fulfillment.

Waiting For Expression
Someone is waiting for you to do what God put in you.

How does it feel like when you accomplish something?
What is it you've stopped dreaming about?
What is it you always wanted to do? (work, etc)
If it doesn't break the bank, will you try it?

---

1. List as many erroneous beliefs as you can.
Ex. I'm not good at math. I'm not artistic.
You'll never be able to do [blank].
[blank] runs in the family. Rich people are evil.

2. Take that list of beliefs and use it to light your fire pit next time you entertain friends/family.
Warning: Be safe, and use caution while playing with fire.

3. Find a friend you trust to become an accountability partner.
You need someone in your corner who can be brutally honest. Someone who can encourage you as you handle those challenges.

You want to stop smoking but keep buying cigarettes.
You want to save but continue buying unnecessary things.
You want to be faithful but keep cheating.
You want to workout but keep flaking on gym days.

The Nursery Principle

I.I.W. - Pro 13:12
Hope deferred makes the heart sick,
but a dream fulfilled is a tree of life.

What is the Nursery Principle? What's that even mean? When a family is having a child they make plans and prepare for the arrival of the child. This happens so fast that you miss the steps of the whole process but still get them done. We don't want to take these moments for granted in the future. So for the rest of this chapter I'd like you to think of the "child" or your "dream" as one and the same. It can be as simple as a new occupation, health, or prosperity.

Make Room

One of the first things expectant parents think about when they discover they're having a child is "Do we have room?" If they have a large home or plenty of space then it's a brief conversation. For others you may have to move some things around and make room or even relocate. But everyone understands that the new child needs room.

The same principle applies for those new dreams and goals we want in our life. You're going to need to shed some old things in order to make room for new things. Trees shed leaves. Dogs shed hair. People shed skin. The old always makes room for the new. When we hold onto things too long we don't allow the new things to come into our life. Some of those things might be people, antiques, or poor thinking; literally and figuratively. All the same, clean it up and clean it out.

Not to sound like a cliché, but…Nature hates a vacuum. Have you ever removed a tree or shrub around the house and within weeks if not days weeds and grass are already growing in the space where you just removed the shrub. It's as if all the other plants were just waiting for you to move that lousy shrub out of the way so they could come in there. Well, in fact that is true. Our ultra-productive creator designed it this way. Nature will never waste an opportunity to grow, and neither should you.

Fill your surroundings with people and things that uplift and encourage you. If none of those things are present you need to make room for what you want in your life. Immediately get rid of things that don't serve your higher purpose. This could mean eliminating some negative relationships. Some people are in your life for a season. Decide if they are there to help or hinder. I've seen God extract so many people from my life that were distractions and time hogs. I no longer question abrupt changes in my life. Whether you pray or meditate, spend some time doing that before you make a decision.

Expectancy

The moment parents see those pregnancy results the wheels start spinning. They picture their life changing, their home changing, their finances changing, and their body changing. Oh, they know there's going to be some changes. Whether the change is good or great they begin setting expectations. Setting expectations is part of the process.

Expectations are a fickle thing, bouncing and changing frequently, and we all have them. Are you anticipating the results you really want? Do you believe those things that line up with your dreams? What we put our faith in *and* focus on we will get in the end. *Faith is a thing*, it's spiritual currency that makes purchases.

Walk in a spirit of expectancy. Les Brown once said "Good things are supposed to happen to me." With an attitude of expectancy things happen. It's as if heaven moves to work favor into your life. If you knew that heaven was moving things around for you why wouldn't you be expectant. Learn to move with an attitude of expectancy.

FOR SOMETHING
NEW TO COME
SOMETHING HAS TO GO

Privacy

There are levels of super secrecy only secret agents and expectant parents know. Expectant parents keep their good news to themselves until they know it's certain. They don't share any news with anyone until they're comfortable. This may be because they don't want misfortune to befall them, or they simply wish to be private because it is a private matter.

Sharing your dream with the wrong people can be catastrophic. If you want to kill a dream, share it with a dream killer. They know just how to kill your dream and make you feel silly for believing you could attain it. The hard part is that these dream killers may be close friends and family which likely means you may actually value their opinion. **So privacy in this case will protect your dream.** The bigger the dream the more protection it needs. Even extroverts need to keep things to themselves at times.

The more you talk about it, the more questions will be asked. The more questions they ask the bigger chance of you speaking something contrary and putting your foot in your mouth. So be prepared for questions but be tactful about what you share. Some dreams are so big they could sound absurd to others and that's ok. If God gave you the dream it's larger than anything you would have come up with on your own.

Preparation

Preparation is the fun part of having a "Child". This is when you have your gender reveals, baby showers, and start your nursery. Essentially designing a place for the baby. This is totally necessary and one of the most creative stages. What would it look like to have no place for the baby? Yeah, not too good.

In the same manner prepare a place for your dream to land. If you're looking for a new wardrobe, clean out your closet or donate some clothing. If you're looking for more possibly get your money affairs in order. Find out how much money you really have. If you're looking for a new car maybe clean out the garage or cleanup the current car so it's ready to go when it's time to go. If you're wanting a new home, clean and decorate your home, or maybe even paint it.

The main point is to be preparing for the old to depart and the new to arrive. You don't need to be specific just very intentional. You have to begin mentally preparing yourself for the blessing. In anticipation of the gift or the blessing make room to receive it.

Words of affirmation and words of faith work wonderfully at this stage. Speaking words of affirmation will quicken your spirit and change your focus. It may seem odd or uncomfortable at first, but stick with it and most importantly *mean what you say*. The only person you need to convince is **yourself**. **If you don't believe anything you say it's a mute point**. You are trying to convince yourself that you deserve whatever it is you're asking for. So be convincing. *Convince yourself.*

Nurture

The baby has to be feed and cared for while it's in the womb and after it's arrival. Just because the baby is born doesn't mean you quit feeding and caring for it.

In order for a dream to grow up big and strong it's gotta be cared for. Feed your dream the right stuff like words of affirmation, faith. And good company is essential. Good company? Yeah, keep all those haters and looky-loos away from your dream or vision. They don't understand it and they don't know how to feed it. Remember to feed your dreams, starve your haters. By all means necessary shield your dream from negativity, yours and others. Don't become discouraged because it's not happening. Your negativity stifles the growth as well.

Thanksgiving & Celebration

Thanksgiving is a two-part event. You should be thankful prior to the "child" or dreams arrival. Then the other instance of Thanksgiving is after you've manifested what you've been waiting for. It's easy to get washed away with emotions in the moment. When it manifests don't neglect to take the time to be thankful for what you waited for.

Thanksgiving

Assert Thanksgiving before the desired dream is present. When you're able to be thankful before receiving the blessing you allow faith to begin working on your behalf. Gratitude assists faith. People are usually grateful after they receive something but fewer are grateful prior to the blessing. Being grateful prior is demonstrating that you have faith that you will receive what you're requesting. Your hope that your request is coming is what Jesus spoke of when he stated "believe that you have received" (Mark 11:23-24). When you show gratitude for things not present the physical world takes back seat to the spiritual.

I.I.W. - Thess 5:18

In everything give thanks: This is the will of God in Christ Jesus concerning you.

Thanksgiving is so powerful! The act of thanksgiving shifts the chemistry in your body. When being thankful the body releases chemicals (dopamine, endorphines, and oxytocin). These chemicals encourage the euphoric feelings you exhibit during moments of gratitude.

Celebration

After you've seen your "child" birthed it's time to party and celebrate. At this phase you can share without cause for privacy. The event you've been planning for has finally arrived and it's beautiful and everything you imagined. Of course you want to share the news! This is what you've been waiting for, *embrace it. Make the necessary adjustments* and ***enjoy the gift!***

MOST FOLKS ARE HAPPY AS THEY MAKE UP THEIR MINDS TO BE.

ABRAHAM LINCOLN

SECTION SUMMARY
Make Room
You need to shed some old things to make room for the new.
The old always makes room for the new.
Fill your surroundings with things that uplift and encourage you.

Expectancy
Walk in a spirit of expectancy.
Learn to move with an attitude of expectancy

Privacy
Sharing your dream with the wrong people can be catastrophic.
Privacy protects your dream.

Preparation
Prepare for the old to depart and the arrival of the new.
The only person you need to convince is yourself.
Words of affirmation will quicken your spirit
and change your focus.

Nurture
Feed your dreams the right stuff.
Shield your dreams from negativity, yours and others.

Thanksgiving & Celebration
Assert Thanksgiving before the desired result is present.
The act of Thanksgiving shifts the chemistry in your body.
Make the necessary adjustments and enjoy the gift!

Has God given you a vision/dream?
Do you believe you can accomplish the dream?
Is it something you can accomplish on your own?
Is it an individual or corporate vision?
Have you shared it with anyone?

Start writing your dreams or visions in your
journal as they are revealed to you.
Be as descriptive as possible.

The Laser Theory

On one occasion I was working through some technical problems I had with a commercial laser I had recently purchased for my home office. I was overwhelmed, frustrated, and sincerely regretting my recent purchase. After numerous calls with technical support I had answered most of my problems. The Tech ended the call commenting "The laser is very violent and powerful. Slow it down. Lower the power, and remember to check your focus!"

I'm always amazed at when and how God chooses to reveal certain things to me. Whether in the kitchen cooking, driving through the forest, working in the garage, and occasionally even during church. I'm always amazed!

Focus

Laser: Think of a laser like a kid playing with a magnifying glass attempting to fry ants, only it's engraving and marking materials. For a laser to be truly effective it has to be focused. The laser can fire and mark materials but the results are sporadic and pretty much a waste of time and materials. To focus the laser you have to align the laser tube and a series of mirrors that lead to the laser head. If any of the mirrors are out of sync the laser hits the laser head out of alignment giving you mixed results. **People:** When we don't focus we get mixed results. If you work in a group where the energy is misaligned; you can tell.

THE RIGHT ENERGY CREATES SYNERGY

Think of the mirrors that align the laser like people that are working together on a project. It helps if you know everyone on your team is capable (meaning they have the power and ability). If your people aren't in sync on a project there's all sorts of disorder. This person is going this direction and another is going the opposite. When two people are pulling in opposing directions it's really hard to get traction in the right direction. Making sure everyone is aligned will ensure that you get the result a little faster!

Power

Laser: The power transmitted through the laser head is tremendous. The CO_2 laser has the ability to engrave and mark stone, wood, and glass in a few seconds. The problem with more power is that the operator has to know when to apply more or less, everything *should not* be engraved at full power. If you use too little power it won't leave a good impression, too much power and it can destroy and burn the materials. **People:** Just as with the laser, the power you exert or demonstrate can help or hurt you. The key is to know when to exert power. If you're trying to move a mountain you can't move it with a spoon - you would just waste valuable time and energy. Likewise, you should not use a bulldozer to move a chair. Knowing when to demonstrate force is key in working with others. There will be times when you need to display power and authority. When power is wielded incorrectly it appears violent and disturbing. We should be humble enough to have an accountability partner that can tell you this without being fearful of retaliation or judgment.

Speed

Laser: That immense power of the laser is coupled with lightning speed, which makes violent moves and jerks since it's moving to make pinpoint precision details. As hyper productive people we tend to think faster is better. If that's the case the ugly results that come from the laser moving too fast must look like the Mona Lisa. Faster is surely not always better. You end up trading off quality for speed in the laser's case. It's alright to slow down, as a result you'll enjoy the results better. **People:** Trading quality and accuracy for rapid completion can lead to poor results. Have you ever seen someone finish something fast and then you wonder if they know how bad it looks? All the while the individual is excited that they completed the task so quickly. Inside you're wishing that they would have just slowed down and took their time. My mother wasn't that easy, once she made me wash the dishes three times. I kept doing them real fast and she kept making me do them over. The same thing plays out when people complete last minute projects (reports, construction projects, etc.) If you would just slow down and give it your focus and attention the end result would be so much better.

Understand The Equipment

Laser: It's highly important for me to know what the laser can and can't do. Without knowing it's limitations I might expect some unreasonable outcomes. Each laser, each brand, is different. I just happen to have this one and I can't expect it to perform exactly like another brand. **People:** Self awareness. Each individual has different "operating parameters". All of our specific attributes give us different capabilities. It doesn't make one of us better than another, just different. Understanding and respecting your given skill set allows you to function ideally at the specific task you were designed for.

End in Mind

If you begin a project without even knowing what you want the end result to look like, you're rushing to failure. But, if you begin your project with the right team in alignment (focused), well rested, prepared, and ready (power), then take the necessary time (speed), you can have the results you envisioned prior to starting the project. This simple philosophy, starting with the end in mind, will help you keep a clear vision. Stay on course so you can see the dream or desired end goal manifest. What are you building and creating? To what purpose?

SECTION SUMMARY

Focus
When we don't focus we get mixed results.
The right energy creates synergy.

Power
Know when to exert power.
Too little power and it won't leave an impression,
Too much power and you destroy and burn.

Speed
It's alright to slow down, you'll enjoy the results better.
Trading quality and accuracy for speed leads to poor results.

Understanding The Equipment
Each individual has different capabilities; respect your skills.

End In Mind
If you begin a project without knowing what you want in
the end result, you're rushing to failure.

Do you work better alone or with a team?
Do you see yourself as an introvert or extrovert?
Do you find it easy to focus on a task?
Are you more of a tortoise or a hare?

Can you recall a group project that went really well?
Can you recall a group project that went badly?
Share what worked in the Great moment.
Share what went wrong in the other.

BEWAR EOFDR EAMKI LLERS

Kingdom
Citizenship

I.I.W - Luke 12:32

Fear not, little flock; for it is your Father's good
pleasure to give you the Kingdom.

Every person has a glimmer of nationalism however acute it may be. Some people may identify as American, Nigerian, English, Indian, etc. but it gets deeper than that as believers. As Believers we have dual citizenship, we are always citizens of two kingdoms, but the kingdom of heaven supersedes all others. This realization changes everything for believers. We are his representatives wherever we go. We are the visual representation of the Kingdom of Heaven.

Ambassadors

When a king sends an ambassador to a foreign land, they always make arrangements prior to the ambassador getting there. While the ambassador is away from home all their needs are still met by the kingdom they serve. So as citizens of heaven your needs should always be met by the Kingdom. All medical needs, financial needs, guidance, orders, and most of all spiritual needs are met by the kingdom.

There is only one kingdom with limitless resources. When your *host country* is dealing with a financial pull-back (recession), it's not the host country's duty to pull you out of it. As a kingdom citizen, the kingdom takes care of its own. The King knows what you need before you ask him (Matt 6:8), but still ask. Jesus shared with the disciples the correct manner in which to pray to the Father. In this you will see The identity, (The Lord is One (Holy), the territory (Thy Kingdom), the request (give us, forgive this, lead us), and the glorification (your kingdom, power, glory). Talk about going right to the source. If you need to know anything about the Father why not ask the Son! The simplicity of this prayer has made it rote, that's not to say it's doesn't work. In it's directness a lot of key points are simply overlooked.

I.I.W. - (Matt 6:9-13)

9After this manner therefore pray ye:
Our Father which art in heaven,
Hallowed (Holy) be thy name.
10THY KINGDOM COME
Thy will be done in earth, as it is in heaven
11Give us this day our daily bread.
12And Forgive us or debts, as we forgive our debtors.
13And lead us not into temptation,
But deliver us from evil:
FOR THINE IS THE KINGDOM,
AND THE POWER,
AND THE GLORY, FOREVER.
Amen.

Resources

In the Prayer above you'll notice the request for provisions. Give us this day our daily bread. Forgive our debts, and lead us not into temptation. Sweet simple and straight to the point. Not begging or pleading in prayer (supplication) just bluntly, give me what I need for today father. It's expressed also in David's 23rd Psalm "The Lord is my shepherd, I shall not want."

As a practice when I need something in prayer whether it be monetary, guidance, or just an ear from heaven I try to remember to present it as a requisition. What? I'm here doing the Lord's work and I need supplies Father, I need guidance, I could use an empathetic car. It may sound weird but isn't it the truth? Our Heavenly Father is also our King. No one goes before the king and wastes his time. So make good use of your time together.

I.I.W. - Num 33:53

And ye shall dispossess the inhabitants of the land, and dwell therein: for I have given you the land to possess it.

Expansion

Every kingdom looks to expand it's borders. As kingdoms prosper, the citizens prosper, the need for more space and territory becomes more of a necessity than a desire. As an ambassador we have a role of great responsibility. We are who the king sends out to scout and acquire new territory. Just as Joshua and Caleb went out to scout the promise land (Num 13:30). We represent the interests of the Kingdom of Heaven's expansion on earth. We have to understand that spiritual colonization is going to happen with or without our participation. The Kingdom of Heaven or The Kingdom of darkness will occupy the land.

The party that rules an area governs that area. **One will occupy the land.** As an ambassador, as a Kingdom advocate, as a Kingdom citizen we don't get to be spectators; this is a engagement exercise. There will be no participation trophy for being on the team. This is a "Ride or Die" event. Get in the car or get out the car. It's going down with or without you. When you don't participate in the colonization you suffer from the wrong kingdom acquiring land and territory. So when you continually see chaos in a city or nation repeatedly you can be sure that spiritual warfare is occurring. *"From the days of John the Baptist until now the kingdom of heaven suffereth violence, and the violent take it by force." Matt 11:12* Just as in the beginning, it was all the Lord's land. You are just taking back what already belongs to your heavenly Father. Amen, "May it be so."

SECTION SUMMARY
Ambassadors
All citizens needs are met by the kingdom they serve.
The King knows what you need even before you ask.

Resources
You don't need to beg and plead every prayer.
Some prayers can be sweet and simple.

Expansion
All kingdoms expand their borders as they prosper.
As ambassadors we participate in kingdom expansion.
We are not spectators, but participants.

What do you see as your role in the Kingdom? Are you a soldier or ambassador?

Scarcity

Stop Accepting Lack

I.I.W. - 3 John 1:2
Beloved, I wish above all things that thou may prosper and be in health, even as thy soul prosper.

No Scarcity - The Kingdom Always Provides

Prosperity was a mandate. *"And God blessed them, and God said unto them, Be fruitful, and multiply, and replenish the earth, and subdue it: and have dominion over the fish of the sea, and over the fowl of the air, and over every living thing that moveth upon the earth."* *(Gen 1:28)* He ordered us to subdue and take dominion of everything on the earth. Note, that he did not tell us to dominate man. We were not given dominion and authority over each other. Those that oppress and overpower their fellow man are doing so of their own will and are out of the will of God.

God has created more than enough resources and wealth on this earth for all of us. Any feeling of lack comes from fear. Fear that God hasn't supplied enough resources. That ideal is not from God.

I.I.W. - Matt 6:8 AMP

[8]So do not be like them [praying as they do]; for your Father knows what you need before you ask Him.

The Kingdom does not function from a position of scarcity, which is why poverty, lack, and illness make us feel so uncomfortable. Poverty is alien to the kingdom and has no authority or place in the kingdom. (Luke 19:12-27) Jesus illustrated in parable a principle of expectancy. Three individuals were given money and two of them increased it but the third saved and held what was given to him. Upon the nobleman's return he asked for an accounting to how much they had increased. The one that didn't increase was severely punished. The Master always expects us to be increasing. "Occupy till I come" (Luke 19:13b)

Jesus Paying Taxes

When in Capernaum, Peter was asked if his master paid tribute (taxes). Jesus immediately responded by asking who do the people of this nation pay tribute to. Jesus stated *"Notwithstanding, less we should offend them, go to the sea, cast a hook, and take up the first fish that comes up; when you open his mouth you should find a piece of money: take that, and give it then to them for you and me."* Matt 17:24-27 Jesus didn't concern himself with money.

He knew where to find money and what to do with it. When confronted on a separate occasion and asked if it was lawful to give Caesar tribute he perceived that they were attempting to entrap him. Jesus responded *"Show me the tribute money. Whose is this image and subscription? Render unto Caesar the things which are Caesar's and unto God the things that are God's."* Matt 22: 17-21

Widow of Zeraphath

Elijah went to Zeraphath as he was commanded. There he had a divine appointment with a widow gathering sticks. He asked her for water and something to eat. She informed him that she had nothing but a handful of meal and a little oil to eat. And was gathering wood so she could make a fire, eat it, and wait for her and her son to die. He commanded her to not fear, go ahead and make the morsel for him and then one for themselves. He assured her that the Lord wouldn't allow the meal to waste, or the oil to fail (until the day the Lord sent rain). Elijah, the widow, and her son ate for many days. (1 Kings 17:10-15)

Food in Exodus

In the wilderness after the exodus from Egypt the people of Israel were starving and thirsty. They began complaining that it would have been better to die back in Egypt than to be dragged into the desert to die of hunger. The Lord responds by raining manna (bread) from heaven in the morning and quails in the evening. They were commanded to gather what they could eat, "some more, some less" and no leftovers, no hoarding. If a portion was leftover it had maggots and stank in the morning. The Lord made a special provision for the sixth day to get a double portion so they would not gather food on the Sabbath. (Exodus 16). The Lord provided for them in this manner for 40 years while they journeyed in the wilderness! (Exodus 16:35)

Even in the midst of grumbling and complaining God sees fit to continue providing food to the Israelites. Have you ever been whiny and seen God bless you in the middle of your pity party? How long is too long to be unappreciative? Jesus may not have been physically present in the Old Testament but his grace was.

Jesus with the Fish and Loaves

After ministering all day to a large gathering in a desert place, the disciples ask Jesus to let them go because it's getting late. Jesus responds *"you give them something to eat"*, and the disciple responds, *"shall we go into town and buy two hundred pennyworth of bread?"* Mark 6: 35-36

We don't know if the disciple was being literal or sarcastic. Keep in mind there are 5,000 men, not including women and children. If they were intending to buy bread for the crowd it needed to be enough to feed 5,000-15,000 people!

Jesus then takes inventory and asks *"How many loaves have you. Go and see."* They return with an account of five loaves and two fish. He commands everyone to sit down on the grass in groups, he takes the food, looks up to heaven, blessed it and hands it to the disciples to distribute. *"They did all eat, and were filled."* Mark 6:38-42

Exodus of Egypt

The Children of Israel were released from bondage after the Passover event where God visited all the houses of Egypt. They were then commanded to leave Egypt with all their flocks and herds and *"be gone"* Exo 12:32. The children of Israel then borrowed the Egyptian's jewels of silver, and jewels of gold, and clothing. The Lord gave them favour in the sight of the Egyptians, so they lent as the children required (Exo 12:35-36). Talk about a severance package! The captors of their 400 year enslavement lent them silver, gold, and clothing as they set them free.

The Kingdom of Heaven always knows how to provide and

The World's Greatest Severance Package

compensate for its citizens. Some may ask why were the children of Israel even in slavery in the first place. Israel's enslavement to Egypt was prophesied hundreds of years prior. It was always part of the plan for God to bless them in that manner. *"And he said unto Abram, Know of a surety that thy seed shall be a stranger in a land that is not theirs, and shall serve them; and they shall afflict them four hundred years; And also that nation, whom they shall serve, will I judge: and afterward shall they come out with substance."* Gen 15:13-14 So after the Exodus you have millions of Israelites trudging through the desert laden with gold, silver, and fine linens and no place to go! **That** is how you make an exit!

Use or Spend

When something is spent it is used till it expires. When something is put into use it's just being utilized or circulated. So the question is do you use money, put it into circulation, or spend money, not looking for it to return? Using something and spending something are not the same.

You spend time. Time is not circulating and does not return. So saying "time is money" is incorrect. You get paid for the value you bring to a situation. If you solve a problem you are being compensated for solving that problem.

If you discovered that you only had another month to live you would pay anything to extend that time. You could acquire more money easily given more time. But you can have unlimited money and can't buy back time. So time in fact is not money but opportunity.

Once while sharing my challenges with growing my business, my father interjected with some "Jedi-like" response. It completely stumped me and had me thinking who is this man, I thought I was talking to my dad. It was like Yoda giving Luke Skywalker advice. It went something like this:

Take a pipe son, filled with water, water should pass through it but never stay in it. If the water sits still it becomes stagnant and it stinks. The pipe is the conduit, it makes sure the water gets from point A to point B. The pipe (you) gets wet but doesn't keep all the water. The water (money) must continue to move and flow, like a current - that's why it's called currency.

We use currency to pay for things. Money should flow through us and circulate. When money is hoarder it doesn't accomplish what it is meant to do; increase and circulate. Money is funny, it likes being around its own kind. Money likes money, which is why those with it have more of it. The law of sowing & reaping is undeniable like the law of gravity. You can use the law; but you can not break the law.

God Boasts on His Servants

God always finds special ways to honor those he considers faithful, righteous, and honorable. God doesn't hold back on details when it comes to describing the accumulated wealth of his faithful servants. God goes into intricate details when he describes a few of them, listing their possession, workers, and family size. Observe the following examples:

Noah

(Gen 6:6) *"It repented the Lord that he had made man on the earth, and it grieved him at his heart"* God then states that he's going to destroy man, beasts, and birds. *"But Noah found grace in the eyes of the lord. These are the generations of Noah: Noah was a **just man** and **perfect in his generations, and Noah walked with God.**"* (Gen 6:8-9) God is going to reset the earth and establish a covenant with Noah. That speaks volumes to how righteous and trustworthy God sees Noah. Noah's wealth never gets mentioned but his personal relationship with God instead.

I.I.W. - Psalm 35:27

Let them shout for joy, and be glad, that favour my righteous cause: yea let them say continually, Let the Lord be magnified, which hath pleasure in the prosperity of his servant.

Abraham

"And Abram was very rich in cattle, in silver, and in gold." Gen 13:2 *"And the land was not able to bear them, that they might dwell together: for their substance was great, so that they could not dwell together."* Gen 13:6 *"And when Abram heard that his brother was taken captive, he armed his trained servants, born in his own house, three hundred and eighteen, and pursued them unto Dan."* Gen 14:14

So here we have Abram who is very wealthy in livestock and precious metals. Abram has so much substance that he and his nephew can no longer occupy the same land. They separate and his nephew Lot gets taken captive. Abram doesn't call for help, he arms 318 of his own armed servants. Abram had enough men in his command to build his own militia. Take that in for a second. In order to warrant the need for 300 strong men he had to have a large substance to take care of and manage. No ordinary cattle or sheep herder by any means.

Job

"There was a man in the land of Uz, whose name was Job; and the man was perfect and upright, and one that feared God, and eschewed evil. And there were born unto him seven sons and three daughters. His substance also was seven thousand sheep, and three thousand camels, and five hundred yoke of oxen, five hundred she asses, and a very great household; so that this man was the greatest of all men of the east" Job 1:3. Job's wealth is immense in comparison then and now. God doesn't restrain any details when describing his servant Job.

The Devil proposes a wager with God; that if he takes everything from Job, that Job will curse him to his face. God allows the devil to test Job, knowing that Job would not blaspheme him.

Job in his many, many, many afflictions, does not curse God. Job is berated and judged by his wife and closest friends. In the midst of his later afflictions he does begin to question God's judgment and righteousness. When this occurs God answers Job appearing in a whirlwind and questions Job. *"Who is it that darkens counsel by words without knowledge?"* (Job 38:2) After God gives Job an earful, Job submits and repents. God then begins the reconciliation. *"¹²So the Lord blessed the latter end of Job more than the beginning: for he had fourteen thousand sheep, and six thousand camels, and a thousand yoke of oxen, and a thousand she asses. ¹³He had also seven sons and three daughters. ¹⁵And in all the land were no women so fair as the daughters of Job: and their father gave them inheritance among their brethren"* (Job 42:12,13,15).

I.I.W. - Isaiah 41:10-11 (ESV)

¹⁰Fear not, for I am with you; be not dismayed, for I am your God. I will strengthen you, I will help you, I will uphold you with my righteous right hand. ¹¹Behold, all who are incensed against you shall be put to shame and confounded; those who strive against you shall be as nothing and shall perish.

I.I.W. - Joshua 1:9
Have I not commanded you? Be strong and courageous. Do not be frightened, and do not be dismayed, for the Lord your God is with you wherever you go.

Recounting Job's ordeal I realized that while an individual is in a distressed spirit it can be difficult to remember that the Lord always wants to bless you. Always remember that God is for us not against us. Surely Job understood this by the end of his trials and testing.

King David & King Solomon
David and Solomon are shining examples of the Kingdom of Heaven's prosperity in action. Since history has done such a fine job of reminding us just how blessed these two kings were I won't burden you with a lengthy account of their riches.

I.I.W. - 2 Chron. 16:9
For the eyes of the Lord run to and fro throughout the whole earth, to shew himself strong on the behalf of them whose heart is perfect toward him.

King David amassed his riches in numerous ways, but these three stand out. *First,* he acquired phenomenal wealth through victorious battle throughout his reign as king. On one account he split the spoils of war with 13 cities. (2 Samuel 30:21-31) *Secondly,* he received tribute. King David reunited Judah and the tribes of Israel and received tribute from Judah, Israel, and a few of the surrounding territories. *Thirdly,* he inherited the possessions of King Saul whom he replaced as king. David reigned 40 years (c. 1010-970 BCE).

King Solomon maintained his inheritance and his wealth continued to grow as other kings and dignitaries would pay tribute and homage to his godly wisdom. King Solomon reigned for 40 years (970-931 BCE), and each year he collected 666 talents of gold, aside from what peddlers and merchants paid in taxation. All of the kings & governors of Arabia brought gold and silver as well. (2 Chron 9:13-14) King Solomon surpassed all the kings of the earth in riches and wisdom. (2 Chron 9:22-23)

God loves to bless his obedient and faithful servants. Those who humble themselves, live their life for service to him; and take his guidance; he blesses generously. God has made these individuals examples so that we would remember and see how good the Lord is. Those that are bountifully blessed are made to be a blessing to others.

SECTION SUMMARY

No Scarcity - The Kingdom Always Provides

God has created more than enough resources for all.
The Kingdom doesn't operate from a position of scarcity.
Prosperity was a mandate.

Use or Spend

Time is not money, but opportunity.
Money should flow through us and circulate.
Money likes being around it's own kind.

God Boasts on His Servants

God finds ways to honor those he considers
faithful and righteous.
Those that are blessed are made to be a blessing to others.
God is for us not against us.

**Do any of these examples stand out to you?
Are there enough resources for everyone?**

Power and Authority

Power and Authority

Jesus told the disciples to wait in Jerusalem, until they were endowed with power from on high (Luke 24:49). That power, The Holy Spirit, also granted them spiritual authority. Since we are grafted into this family, we too are granted the same power and authority. It's extremely humbling to know that we are the chosen vessel that the Father created to demonstrate his power and authority.

Imagine a police officer walking into the street and waving his hand to stop traffic. As the officer steps off the curb some cars immediately come to a halt and others shortly proceed afterwards. That is what authority looks like. Without saying anything the uniform reminded the people who they were dealing with. In case someone wants to question his authority the officer can display his badge to remind those in opposition. Frequently, there are those that oppose that authority. On that occasion, the officer needs to demonstrate force or fire power.

²And when he was come out of the ship, immediately there met him out of the tombs a man with an **unclean spirit**, ➡ ⁶But when he saw Jesus afar off, he ran and **worshiped him**, ⁷and cried with a loud voice, and said, <u>What have I to do with thee</u>, Jesus, thou Son of the most high God? <u>I adjure thee</u> by God, <u>that thou torment me not</u>. ⁸For he said unto him, Come out of the man, thou unclean spirit. ⁹And he asked him, What is thy name? And he answered, saying, My name is Legion: for we are many. ¹⁰And he **besought him** much that he would not **send them away out of the country**. ¹¹Now there was there nigh unto the mountains a great herd of swine feeding. ¹²And all the devils besought him, saying, Send us into the swine, that we may enter into them. ¹³And forthwith <u>Jesus gave them leave</u>. And the unclean spirits went out, and entered into the swine: and the herd ran violently down a steep place into the sea, (**they were about two thousand**;) and were choked in the sea.

Jesus has just calmed a storm and is immediately met with a man possessed with an *unclean spirit*. The first thing the unclean spirit does is begin worshiping Jesus, and crying out "What do I have to do with you?" The spirit also calls Jesus the "Son of God". At that point that was not known by anyone. Then, the spirit pleads with Jesus. "I beg you, please don't torment me." Jesus commands the spirit to come out of the man, and the spirit reveals its name, Legion. Once again the spirit pleads to not be sent out of the territory. The spirit knows it's going to be expelled out of the host. The greatest concern now is that it doesn't want to lose the territory it's been occupying. For the third time the spirit pleads to be cast into a herd of swine.

Jesus grants them leave. You can see a spiritual hierarchy here. The spirit is continually pleading (three times), and Jesus is holding court, he casts the spirit into a herd of swine. Spirits have to have hosts. The herd of swine run violently down the hill and drown in the sea. Then we discover there were two thousand spirits in the man. The havoc those two thousand spirits could have potentially unleashed would have been catastrophic if those swine had lived. Jesus appearing in that town was an appointment.

SPIRITUAL GIFTS

When you deploy a soldier on a battlefield you give them the tools and weapons to succeed. The godhead has done that as well. The Holy Spirit is the "Multi-tool of the body of Christ"

I.I.W. - Acts 2:2-4

And suddenly there came a <u>sound</u> from heaven as of a rushing mighty wind, and it filled all the house where they were sitting. And there appeared unto them cloven <u>tongues</u> like as of fire, and sat upon each of them. And they were all filled with the Holy Ghost, and began to <u>speak</u> with other <u>tongues</u>, as the Spirit gave them <u>utterance</u>.

*Cloven: divided in two, separated.

Before Jesus departed he commanded them to wait until the comforter come; that would gift them with *power from on high* (Luke 24:49). When the Holy spirit arrived to the people in the upper room the first demonstration was tongues, but the spirit brought eight other gifts as well. *⁴Now there are diversities of gifts, but the same Spirit. ⁵And there are differences of administrations, but the same Lord. ⁶And there are diversities of operations, but it is the same God which worketh all in all. ⁷But the manifestation of the Spirit is given to every man to profit withal. ⁸For to one is given by the Spirit the <u>word of wisdom</u>; to another the <u>word of knowledge</u> by the same Spirit; ⁹to another <u>faith</u> by the same Spirit; to another the <u>gifts of healing</u> by the same Spirit; ¹⁰to another the <u>working of miracles</u>; to another <u>prophecy</u>; to another <u>discerning of spirits</u>; to another <u>divers kinds of tongues</u>; to another the <u>interpretation of tongues</u>: ¹¹but all these worketh that one and the selfsame Spirit, dividing to every man severally as he will.(1 Corin 12:4-11)*

Jesus made it abundantly clear that they were not to depart until the spirit came. He wanted them to have these gifts, all of them! Why then do we see some segments or denominations of Christianity not using the gifts of the spirit and some even rejecting them.

When Jesus selected the disciples he was aware of their differences. They didn't always get along and at times argued who would be the greatest amongst them (Mark 9:33-36). That argument seems to still carry on. The one thing the disciples and followers of that day did do correctly was assemble regardless of differences and activate the gifts of the spirit. They understood that they were more effective together.

The need for that unity is upon us at this day and time as well. Now more than ever the kingdom of darkness is pressing against us. If we don't present a unified front we're not as effective as God needs us to be. *¹²For as the body is one, and hath many members, and all the members of that one body, being many, are one body: so also is Christ. ¹³For by one Spirit are we all baptized into one body, whether we be Jews or Gentiles, whether we be bond or free; and have been all made to drink into one Spirit. ¹⁴For the body is not one member, but many. ¹⁵If the foot shall say, Because I am not the hand, I am not of the body; is it therefore not of the body? ¹⁶And if the ear shall say, Because I am not the eye, I am not of the body; is it therefore not of the body? ¹⁷If the whole body were an eye, where were the hearing? If the whole were hearing, where were the smelling? ¹⁸But now hath God set the members every one of them in the body, as it hath pleased him. 1 Corinthians 12:12-18*

We are THE BODY OF CHRIST, not just members! Some are called to teach, preach, and others evangelism. Until we embrace this truth we won't be able to complete the task commissioned to us. *"Every kingdom divided against itself is brought to desolation; and every city or house divided against itself shall not stand: Matt 12:25*

As awkward and difficult as it may be to share our faith in the work place we should take every opportunity to advance the word and knowledge of God. For some of us this may be more challenging but still stay about the Father's business. The Holy Spirit will provide opportunities for this to happen. Ask in prayer how to do such.

Each of our talents and gifting allow us access to different people daily. We don't need to be a pop star or athlete to get an audience with someone who needs God's help. God knows this, which is why there are so many different gifts. One person's gift of healing is no different than another person's gift of word of wisdom or word of knowledge. Each gifting provides an "in" for the Holy spirit to act upon someone's life. By embracing our uniqueness and willingly activating our gift we can accomplish what the Kingdom needs us to do.

Opposition From Spiritual Forces

Just as police officers are continuously challenged by criminal adversaries, believers are stricken with the same calamity. A policeman or soldier are quickly spotted by their uniform. Believers are identified by the spiritual persona they emit and calling God places on them. Once principalities see you as a threat to their agenda you are targeted more frequently. The closer you draw to God the more of a threat you pose. *"Be sober, be vigilant; because your adversary the devil, as a roaring lion, walketh about, seeking whom he may devour" 1Pet 5:8, Job 1:7*

The enemy is always looking to kill your dreams, your purpose, your calling; kill your will, and even kill you. This I tell you to arm you, not startle and scare you. Don't be misguided to think you can challenge and combat these powers in your own strength. In order to take the offensive you have to be imbued with powers from on high. You need to be walking in the anointing. The spiritual realm can see your spiritual expertise. Don't bring a knife to a gun fight.

I.I.W. - Acts 19:11-16

And God wrought special miracles by the hands of Paul: [12]so that from his body were brought unto the sick handkerchiefs or aprons, and the diseases departed from them, and the evil spirits went out of them. [13]Then certain of the vagabond Jews, exorcists, took upon them to call over them which had evil spirits the name of the Lord Jesus, saying, We adjure you by Jesus whom Paul preacheth. [14]And there were seven sons of one Sceva, a Jew, and chief of the priests, which did so. [15]And the evil spirit answered and said, **Jesus I know, and Paul I know; but who are ye?** [16]And the man in whom the evil spirit was leaped on them, and overcame them, and prevailed against them, so that they fled out of that house naked and wounded.

Several things happened in this passage. First, Paul's clothes were so imbued with the holy spirit that his garments carried the anointing. People were being healed by just touching his clothing articles. His clothing cast out evil spirits! Secondly, those witnessing the event felt empowered enough to begin the same casting out because they believed they could do the same. Brave, yes. Motivated, yes. Smart, not really.

Finally, the spirits immediately perceived they could overthrow them. The spirits then attacked them and overcame them and they fled wounded and naked. Principalities can see how strong your anointing and relationship with God is. DO NOT go into spiritual warfare willy-nilly (haphazardly). Look at Jesus' response to a spiritual attack (below). Jesus is baptized and immediately he is tempted in the wilderness. How does Jesus respond?

I.I.W. - Matt 4:1-11 (NIV)
(First Challenge)

¹Then <u>Jesus was led by the Spirit into the wilderness to be tempted by the devil.</u> ²After fasting forty days and forty nights, he was hungry. ³The tempter came to him and said, "If you are the Son of God, tell these stones to become bread." ⁴Jesus answered, **"It is written: Man shall not live on bread alone, but on** every word that comes from the mouth of God."

(Second Challenge)

⁵Then the devil took him to the holy city and had him stand on the highest point of the temple. ⁶"If you are the Son of God," he said, "throw yourself down. For it is written: "He will command his angels concerning you, and they will lift you up in their hands, so that you will not strike your foot against a stone." ⁷Jesus answered him, **"It is also written: Do not put the Lord your God to the test."**

(Third Challenge)

⁸Again, the devil took him to a very high mountain and showed him all the kingdoms of the world and their splendor. ⁹"All this I will give you," he said, "if you will bow down and worship me." ¹⁰Jesus said to him, **"Away from me, Satan! For it is written: Worship the Lord your God, and serve him only."** ¹¹Then the devil left him, and angels came and attended him.

Two Kingdoms Have a Cease Fire

Jesus has just been baptized and is ushered into the wilderness and immediately the devil starts the inquisition. Knowing that Jesus has been fasting for 40 days, the devil suggests for him to turn stones into bread. Jesus does not, but replies with the word of God.

"It is written: Man shall not live on bread alone, but on every word that comes from the mouth of God." Deut 8:3 The devil then takes him to the holy city on top of the the the temple and dares him to throw himself down.

"For it is written: He will command his angels concerning you, and they will lift you up in their hands, so that you will not strike your foot against a stone." Psalm 91:11-12 Here I noticed two things. The accuser of the brethren, the devil, likes to test people and he knows the word of God. We do not have to prove anything to the kingdom of darkness. It's not our job to prove anything. The law has already been written; we just need to know it. Jesus replies again with the word.

"It is also written: Do not put the Lord your God to the test." Deut 6:16 Finally the devil takes Jesus to a high mountain and shows Jesus all of the world and offers it to him if he will just bow down to him in worship. At this point Jesus has had enough and he rebukes the devil. *"Away from me, Satan! For it is written: Worship the Lord your God, and serve him only." Deut 6:13*

This is also noteworthy, all of Jesus' rebuttals come from the 2nd book of the law, Deuteronomy. Jesus has just given a masterclass on how to handle the accuser of the brethren. Last, but not least, the devil then left him and the angels came to attend to Jesus. (I hope they brought food), (Matt 4:2) the messiah was hungry.

Jesus is the fulfillment of the law not the removal of the law. (Matt 5:17-20) We are saved by grace, but as a citizen of the Kingdom we should still know and understand the laws even if we have been pardoned from them. The enemy is beguiling. Knowing the law also keeps you protected from deception. *"[8]This Book of the Law shall not depart from your mouth, but you shall meditate on it day and night, so that you may be careful to do according to all that is written in it. For then you will make your way prosperous, and then you will have good success. [9]Have not I commanded thee? Be Strong and of good courage; be not afraid, neither be thou dismayed: for the LORD thy God is with thee whither soever thou goest." Josh 1:8-9*

For His Glory

Jesus, the Messiah, stated *"If you abide in me, and my words abide in you, you can ask what you will, and it shall be done unto you. Herein is my father glorified, that you bear much fruit; and so you shall be my disciples."* *John 15:7-8* Our authority and power are the result of our relationship with the Son. Jesus is entrusting us with the power that the Father has allowed him to release unto us disciples! We are given access to the Kingdom by and through Jesus The Christ. All things in this life and the next are for the glory of God.

I.I.W. - Eph 6:12

For we wrestle not against flesh and blood, but against principalities, against powers, against the rulers of the darkness of this world, against spiritual wickedness in high places.

FAMILY · RELIGION · EDUCATION · MEDIA · ENTERTAINMENT · BUSINESS · GOVERNMENT

These principalities mentioned in Ephesians 6 are set in pivotal positions of control and influence. Dominionism is uprooting these principalities and placing God back in charge by instituting a world that is led and governed by believers. Some individuals believe that believers only want to be in control of all the resources. That would be correct but not the entire reason. Why would we want evil to be in control of everything? Where the spirit of the Lord is, there is freedom (2 Cor 3:17), It just makes sense that the Kingdom steward those.

Built For This

As someone who has overcome self sabotage & family addictions, I know what evil is out there. I have literally been thrown from a tank, and nearly run over by a car, and other near misses. The enemy has been out to get me for some time. BUT GOD. I now know my purpose, so all the chaos finally makes sense. (Rom 8:28)

So many "good people" are sheltered. When great sin and spiritual adversity come we don't always see it. When you were saved, it was a win! I know I was a win! I shared with a pastoral friend of mine that I didn't envy him. He was saved, committed his life, and married at a young age. If sin in its many facets was to come upon him, he might not see it coming. Me on the other hand, I've witnessed sin played out in so many ways that my exposure to it has informed me what to look for. Glory to God. I was built for this fight.

Change of Command

Mark 9:2-13; Matt 17:1-13; Luke 9:28-36

John, Peter, and James are taken with Jesus to go pray. As Jesus begins to pray his countenance is changed and he and his clothing appear white and glistening. Moses and Elijah (Elias) appear and are speaking with Jesus. Peter shouts out to Jesus that they should build three tabernacles (alters) one for Jesus, one for Moses, and one for Elijah. While Peter is speaking, the voice of God from a cloud speaks, "This is my beloved son: Hear him", and when they looked around all they see is Jesus.

Jesus then instructs them to not speak of this event until after he has risen from the dead. This becomes known as the Mount of Transfiguration. The disciples question among themselves what he meant about his death.

I.I.W. - 5:17-18

17 Think not that I am come to destroy the law, or the prophets: I am not come to destroy, but to fulfill. 18For verily I say unto you, Till heaven and earth pass, one jot or one tittle shall in no wise pass from the law, till all be fulfilled.

This event is akin to a presidential inauguration ceremony or military Change of Command ceremony. Moses and Elijah (Elias) are transferring power. They are passing the baton. Moses represents the Law, and Elias represents the prophets. This is why Jesus always references "The Law and the Prophets" he's alluding to the upcoming transfer of authority and power.

Only one other moment comes to mind when God's spirit made someone shine. When Moses was with God and came down to give the people the law his face was shining and he didn't even know it. Aaron and the other people of Israel were afraid to come near him. (Exodus 34:29-30)

Jesus is the fulfillment of the law. He did not come to remove the law but to create a bridge between man and God. *Jeremiah 30:33 "but this shall be the covenant that I will make with the house of Israel; After those days, saith the LORD, I will put my law in their inward parts, and write it in their hearts; and will be their God, and they shall be my people."* Once again Jesus is fulfilling another prophecy and bridging the gap.

SECTION SUMMARY
Power and Authority
We are granted power and authority through Jesus.

Spiritual Gifts
Diversity of gifts and differences of administration
A kingdom divided against itself can't stand.
Our different gifts allow us access to different people.

Opposition From Spiritual Forces
The closer you draw to God the more of a threat you pose.
You can not challenge these powers in your own strength.
The spiritual realm can see your spiritual expertise.

Two Kingdoms Have a Cease Fire
You do not need to prove anything to the accuser.
Knowing the law keeps you protected from deception.
The Devil knows the word.

For His Glory
All things are for the Glory of God.
Our authority and power are the result of our
relationship with Jesus, the Messiah.

Change of Command
The Mount of Transfiguration was a Change of Command.
Jesus is the fulfillment of the Law and Prophets.
Jesus came to bridge the gap between man and God.

Have you identified your spiritual gift?
What do you see as your spiritual gifting?
Are you able to share your faith and the word openly?
If it doesn't break the bank, will you try it?

....

In your prayer time ask for opportunities to share your
faith and the word of God. (Not preach, just share.)

Producers
Make The World Go Round

I.I.W. - Eccl. 9:10
"Whatsoever thy hand findeth to do, do it with thy
might; for there is no work, nor device, nor knowledge,
nor wisdom, in the grave, where thou goest."

The Kingdom Raises Producers

The Kingdom of Heaven always raises producers. The Kingdom has to. As the King sets the standard, productivity is rewarded and even required from its citizens. God is not happy with dead weight.

The largest measure of a kingdom's wealth is measuring how much it produces, also referred to as GDP. A nation having wealth and not producing anything to trade, sell, or barter will cannibalize itself. It's human nature to consume, but what's consumed must be replenished. Producers bring value to the marketplace. It's also the reason businesses and corporations are taxed differently than individual employees. Governing bodies understand that without producers an economy will grind to a halt. So, a productive system will promote business growth and help those businesses.

Producers provide to the rest of God's kingdom. They understand that they serve a larger purpose, the masses. Even in the secular community this is recognized. The greater your compensation, the more people you serve. This is quite evident when you look at the people behind the largest corporations. None of those companies get that large serving a small community. The more you serve the larger you need to be.

A MAN'S GIFT
MAKETH
ROOM FOR HIM,
& BRINGETH
HIM BEFORE
GREAT MEN.
PROVERBS 18:16

In 2021, of the top 20 wealthiest people in the world, 13 of the 20 were Americans. The other 7 came from France, Mexico, India, China, and Spain. India produced 40% of the worlds cotton (#2 China, #3 US). The US produced 20% of the world's oil. Texas produces 43% of US oil and 40% of US cotton.

Kingdom Promotion

When God identifies a producer that's a superb manager he promotes them violently! God knows how to manage, and he will disrupt the existing condition of things; his autonomy affords him this. When you've created everything from scratch you know how it's supposed to function and you work with it's tendencies. So, at times violent changes are needed and God does just that.

Prison to Palace

Young Joseph is betrayed by his brothers, but instead of killing him they trade him into slavery. In his servitude he is accused of assault and thrown into prison. In prison he befriends a baker who forgets about him but later remembers that Joseph can decipher dreams. Joseph reveals the meaning of Pharaohs' dreams and being pleased with the interpretation he appoints Joseph second in command of Egypt. Josephs guidance carries Egypt through a seven year famine.

Orphan to Prince

Moses was born under an Egyptian decree ordering Hebrew male children born be slain. He was abandoned in a basket and left in the reeds alongside a river. The pharaoh's daughter finds Moses and having *"compassion"* she adopts Moses as her own. Moses is raised, instructed, and provided for as one of the Egyptian royalty. After Moses commits murder defending a slave he flees. He abandoned everything he knew and lived in exile for thirty years. Moses returns only to demand release of the enslaved Israelites in Pharaohs care.

Farm Field to Battle Field

King David was born a shepherd and had no formal training in royal courts or the battlefield, yet was anointed by God through the prophet Samuel to precede the current king. The day he volunteered to quiet the combatant, Goliath, that had taunted his nation for 40 days, he was thrust into history. David without a helmet, armor, or a sword bested a tested warrior with a slingshot and a rock.

Afterwards he was embraced by King Saul, then chased for eight years. Eventually David reigned over and united Judea and Israel. The man who formally lead sheep now lead soldiers.

Though these examples may be popular they are not exclusive. God continues to appoint and anoint champions who have proven their heart worthy towards him. His favor has been spread abroad to believers & unbelievers. The greatest defining quality seems to be that he trust you with what he needs you to accomplish. God is the manager of managers.

Stewardship

Stewardship and management are coupled together. You can be a manager and not be a steward, though you should be. As well as you could be a phenomenal steward and not be a manager in title. Stewardship means that you oversee and take care of "things" on God's behalf. As a steward nothing is yours. Your every action and motivation is to take care of your master's property. Our heavenly Father being our master, and everything around us being His, we are *inclined* to look after it all. ***We didn't create it, we are the caretakers of it!*** (Genesis 2:15) You don't have to be into animal husbandry, agriculture, farming, and science to be a steward. Stewardship duties are all around you.

Our unhealthy obsession with possessions is nothing new. For centuries people have been feebly trying to take possessions from this life into the next. Always attempting to bury themselves with trinkets that someone later comes and acquires. This is akin to a toddler with a toy crying "mine, mine, mine" only to be separated from it later.

Honestly, I understand it's great having things but we don't need to grow so attached to things that it becomes a compulsion. We won't be taking these things with us and they aren't the reason for our existence here anyway. All that we acquire only helps those that come after us not having to start from scratch.

If your employee kept acting like everything you owned was his, wouldn't you fire them eventually? Our master doesn't do this because He's a gracious master. If our stewardship mutates into ownership we have a *grave* problem. When we start believing that we own anything here on this planet, we've lost sense of our greater purpose. That's a problem.

As a solopreneur business owner it's easy to become prideful and feel like the wealth I have originated with me. Over time I've noticed that when I focus on the sale and not the individuals I'm serving, God has a unique way of slowing things down. I know that my ABBA is not being punitive but keeping me accountable. My prayer for business has always been for Him to bless me as I make myself a blessing. I also ask that the prosperity not ruin me or change me. That's not the case for everyone but I remember when I started my business and what my prayer was. I wanted to serve people and be a part of their business growth and because of that I've assisted some great businesses for over a decade.

Stewardship should include your time, money, and relationships as well. God is very big on relationships. He wants use to work and live cohesively together. Stewarding your time sounds weird, but actually it isn't. One of people's biggest complaints are, "There's just not enough time." Everyone gets the same 24 hours. If you're intentional and mindful of your time you can get the most out of it. We see highly successful people and wonder how they accomplish so many things. Those people are very intentional with their time. "Waste not, want not!"

Relationships are how things get done faster. When you "know the right people" things just happen quickly or "fall in your lap." When you are in unproductive relationships you are essentially wasting time. Not wanting to come off harsh, but this is a simple truth. We all know people who harp and complain every time you see them, that is until, you make it a point to quit running into them. We all have the same 24 hours. You must decide how you'll use yours. Nurture and care for healthy relationships. Relationships are an investment in time and love. If you haven't deposited any time and love into a friendship/marriage you don't get to make a regular withdrawal. You are delinquent of funds, you're withdrawals are bigger than your deposits.

Murmuring and complaining is being a poor steward. *'Do all things without grumbling or disputing" Phil 2:14 ESV* When you complain, you're telling God, "I can't work out this situation Father so I'm going to whine and complain about it". He wants you to make yourself available to Him so He can do something about it. We are his body, we do the walking and talking. *"for it is God who works in you, both to will and to work for his good pleasure." Phil 2:13*

The Only Time Jesus Cursed Anything

Jesus and the disciples are walking leaving Bethany returning to Jerusalem. When he comes upon a fig tree with leaves but no fruit. Jesus curses it *"May no one ever eat your fruit again!" (Mark 11:12-14 NLT)* He completes what he was going to Jerusalem to do and in the evening passing back by the tree the disciples notice the tree is withered and dead.

This may seem harsh or uncalled for but Jesus displayed a strong principle. The Kingdom expects everything in it to produce; in season and out of season. When products of the Kingdom aren't producing they're out of his will. As previously stated everything God creates needs to produce. That's the way He's designed everything. God *doesn't like* to micromanage his creations. Untainted all His works should function, & produce as designed. Though that's not always the case.

The other thing Jesus was silently demonstrating was that all of creation should recognize the creator. *"I tell you that, If these should (people) hold their peace, the stones would immediately cry out." Luke 19:40b* The Godhead's physical manifestation has just come visiting and you have nothing for him! All of creation knows its creator.

We have all been guilty of "looking busy" or productive. The telltale is if the busyness is producing the desired result. Some of us are just busy for the sake of being busy. It looks good, "has leaves", but is bearing no fruit. *John 15:2 "Every branch in me that beareth not fruit he taketh away: and every branch that beareth fruit, he purgeth it, that it may bring forth more fruit."*

Next time you go grocery shopping I want you to note what section the fruits and vegetables come from. Last time I checked you find the fruits and vegetables in the *Produce section*. LOL. God is so wonderful. He can give revelation out of anything.

I.I.W. - (GEN 1:28)

God blessed them, and God said unto them, be fruitful, and multiply, and replenish the earth and subdue it.

GOD IS LOOKING FOR A RETURN

I.I.W. - (Matt 25:14-30)

Thou wicked and slothful servant, thou knewest that I reap where I sowed not, and gather where I have not strawed.

....

The Rewards of Productivity & Consistency

When Job, Abraham, David, Solomon, Jacob, and Noah are mentioned, the Bible never omits the size of their territories, physical possessions, or their workforce and families provided for. They were in charge of vastly more than the average person.

Productivity

God is in the business of productive creation. Nature flourishes, wildlife reproduces, the weather runs its cycle, one season ushering in the next. Just as in nature, it is the same for mankind. In the garden he directed Adam to manage the garden. Adam went about naming and conducting himself and God saw Adam needing a help mate and created woman. From the onset of time God knew that Adam, the first godly manager, was going to need a helper. God uses the obscure and unqualified; God manages great managers. That's what he does. He's proven this numerous times over countless millennia.

God unselfishly rewards productive managers, saved and unsaved. The law of productivity like the Law of gravity has no bias.

I.I.W - Luke 12:48b esv

For everyone to whom much is given, from him much will be required; and to whom much has been committed, of him they will ask the more.

Consistency

Doing the same thing *incorrectly* and expecting different results may be insanity. But, doing the right thing, *the right way* multiple times is progress. When you find the manner that gets the best results and you continue to replicate it that endeavor yields tremendous results in your favor. God knows how to reward consistency; so does the world. So many people are inconsistent to the point that when consistency and dependability are identified they are rewarded in large amounts for the value they bring.

I personally despise the term "Overnight Success"; it's akin to a backhanded compliment. When people use this term in reference to a person's success they are minimizing the work and patience someone has put into a work. Seeing the fruit of someone's labor and passion never reveals the countless time and work they've put into it. Joseph would have been considered an overnight success if we didn't know the history behind his rise to promotion (Genesis 41:37-57). He had to withstand his circumstances for more than 13 years. If a business took 13 years to become what most consider successful the person running the business does not feel like it was overnight at all. He was there from Day 1. They eat, sleep, and drink that business. Don't minimize someone's sacrifice.

How Do You Manage

The way we handle situations will dictate how we get promoted in God's Kingdom. God is so situational. The Kingdom is always looking at how we manage situations, resources, and our integrity. All things come to light. *Situations:* Do you inquire counsel from God? Do you seek counsel from others better suited to help you? Do you panic or stay calm? *Resources:* Can you motivate yourself? Do you motivate others? Do you demonstrate gratitude? Do you make lemonade from lemons? *Home life:* Is there a spiritual/home/work balance? *Integrity:* Do you demonstrate integrity even when no one is looking? Do you make decisions that will benefit others? Do you make yourself accountable to others?

Things People Say About Money

People say a lot about money, but I've realized that says more about their relationship with money than anything else. I myself know and understand money has a powerful spirit behind it. More decisions are made based on money than anything else. Just think about it. Talking about money in public has been as ill advised as talking about politics. People have money wounds just like they have church wounds. In America, money is one of the top 3 reasons that couples disagree or argue, and one of the top 10 reasons for divorce.

"Money isn't important"

We intentionally use *more than* a third of our life at work, the large majority of it, working for someone else. These employers, however benevolent, are in essence paying for your life, if we're being honest. So, money *is important* and as long as you feel that way it will manage to continue sliding through your hands. Those that handle large amounts of it know this and honor money with the decisions they make in putting it to use. Money is the hammer that drives the nail. It takes both to build a house.

True money isn't everything but it will allow you to move freely without barriers so that you can accomplish the things that God needs you to do as well as some of the things you'd like to do. Having money will allow you to give generously without worrying if your needs are met. It will allow you to spend more time with your loved ones if you choose also. Money is a thing! (Matt 6:33)

"Money is the root of all evil"

No, loving money more than God, each other, or ourselves is evil. (1 Tim 6:10) Money in and of itself is only a magnifier of the person that possesses it. The lack of money produces just as much fear and evil. Scarcity is not a kingdom state of mind. God's Kingdom doesn't acknowledge lack. More crime is committed by people looking to obtain more money than by people who have it. Yes, you have rich swindlers, but there are poor swindlers as well. Don't let one criminal represent a whole class of wealth.

Money is the only tangible thing Jesus ever compared to God in reference to serving. He never compared lust, envy, pride, or greed on par with God (Luke 16:13). But he did compare money to God. Money has a spirit to it. When you have money you're in an elevated state; when you lack it and need it, you're placed in a lowly state. The discomfort someone feels from the lack is a signal that something is off. The Kingdom does not function in lack or scarcity.

God Has no problem with you having money, Just don't let your Money have You

All hard work brings a profit, but mere talk leads only to poverty.

Work For A Wage

The reality for some of us is that our current occupation may not be glamorous or even fulfilling. But we would be wise to remember *"Whatever we do, in word or deed, do it unto the Lord and not unto men." Col 3:17a* The individual who is faithful in a little can be trusted with much more. (Luke 16:10).

If we whine and bellyache about the work we currently perform, we're sending the Father the wrong feedback. If, instead we demonstrated hard-work, gratitude, and thanksgiving; we would create an environment for the new opportunity and the Father to bless. Why would our heavenly Father want to give something better and greater to a complaining child? Does that work with our children?

Be thankful for a job you can perform and a Father providing for you and your family. If it's your first job or last, do it diligently and happily as if it were unto the Lord. If you seek to get out of it then ask Him how you transition from this job to the next. But complaining will not get you anywhere with your circumstances or with God.

I.I.W. - 3 John 1:2

Beloved, I wish above all things that thou may prosper and be in health, even as thy soul prosper.

STRAY THOUGHT. CHEW ON THIS..

In my yard I get an instant visualization of productivity and prosperity on display constantly with pine trees on my property. Some years our evergreens grow leaps and bounds and other seasons in small unnoticeable increments. Evergreens continue growth even in their dormant season during the winter conserving energy waiting for the Spring and Summer to come. But they NEVER stop growing. What can we learn from that?

Do we just give up when conditions aren't like we'd like them? When we don't get what we need do we dig deeper or pull up roots *(retard progress)* and just die, *figuratively?*

Trees don't need people to come fertilize them, *(at least not mature trees).* Everything they need is readily available to them. Take for instance, we live in the Rocky Mountain region. No one is going to fertilize those trees in the wilderness. If you ever talk to an arborist they may tell you fertilizing can be dangerous in some cases and may actually harm a tree.

The fertilization could give the tree a dependency. The tree will look for this outer stimulation and can no longer function fully on its own or won't work to dig it's roots down deeper and search for the nutrients. The tree becomes lazy!

SECTION SUMMARY

The Kingdom Raises Producers
Producers provide to the rest of God's kingdom.
Producers bring value to the marketplace.

Kingdom Promotion
God violently promotes superb managers.
God is a manager of managers.

Stewardship
A steward is an overseer for a master.
Stewardship should not turn into ownership.
As a steward nothing is yours.
God is looking for a return.

The Rewards of Productivity & Consistency
God manages managers.
Consistency is valuable and is rewarded.
Overnight success is not a compliment.

How Do You Manage
How we handle things dictates promotion in the Kingdom.

Things People Say About Money

Work For a Wage
Whatever we do, do as unto the Lord
Bring honor to the work of your hands.

Do you see yourself as a steward?
Do you see the value you bring to your job?
In the parable of the talents, which are you?
Do you have false beliefs about money?
If so, where do you feel they came from?

Answer the questions in "How Do You Manage"
Situations/Home life/Resources/Integrity

Identity
More Than You Think

When it comes to identity we need to erase some of the things we taught ourselves about ourselves. Unless of course, it's serving you very well. For a larger majority of us some of those ideals don't serve us all that well; and we deserve better. God doesn't make junk regardless of what you may have experienced or heard. God, the Creator, doesn't make mistakes. Even injuries are for His glorification (John 9:2-3). Who you are in Him, with Him, because of Him, in His Kingdom is what you should be concerned with. God took painstaking measures to create each and everyone of us. We should bask in that fact and enjoy our uniqueness. The dreams He placed in you, He never planned for someone else to do. However, He will find someone else to accomplish the task if you don't accept.

I.I.W. - Psalms 8:4-6
⁴What is man, that thou art mindful of him?
And the son of man, that thou visitest him?
⁵For thou hast made him a little lower than angels,
And hast crowned him with glory and honour.
⁶Thou madest him to have dominion over the works of
thy hands; Thou hast put all things under his feet:

Our current culture would have us believe that our occupation, gender, country of origin, age, and cultural people group are what define our identity. Those are significant markers but that's not how God identifies us. Our identity is much more complex and divine than that. God literally formed us from the earth and breathed life into us. The other creations He spoke into life. *"then the Lord God formed the man of dust from the ground and breathed into his nostrils the breath of life, and the man became a living creature." Gen 2:7*

We literally carry God's breath in us. Ruahk: breath, spirit, wind. The term human means formed from the earth. So we are essentially spirit filled beings formed from the earth. Take one moment…Spirit filled being formed from the earth. Pop culture coined the term science fiction but God is the manifestation of *science-fact*. Look at yourself like a unicorn because, Hey you're magical!

We have the distinction to communicate and create. No other creation has 100's of languages or creates different habitats based on location. We move freely about overseeing all the creations that came before us. We are the upgrade! We simply need to start behaving like we were designed. We are who He says we are. *John 15:15 "Henceforth I call you not servants; for the servant knoweth not what his lord doeth: but I have called you friends; for all things that I have heard of my Father I have made known unto you."* The rest of creation doesn't call upon the Father for counsel or have a relationship with the Creator. We didn't chose Him, He chose us. Adam walked with Him in conversation and communion in The Garden of Eden.

With all of our intellect, science, and sorted emotions; we have over complicated the simplicity of our identity. You were formed from the supernatural, so be that. Be Supernatural, His spirit lives in us! Lions hunt, fish swim, and eagles fly. At whatever level He's designated you to be at currently; do what he assigned you to do; steward, grow, teach, preach, love, govern and grow.

Jesus: *[15]I know thy works, that thou art neither cold nor hot: I would thou wert cold or hot. [16]So then because thou art lukewarm, and neither cold nor hot, I will spue thee out of my mouth. (Rev 3-16,17)* Whatever you do though, do it to the maximum with his love and righteousness. He didn't halfway create the universe! When you put your hands to it leave your mark on it, just like he left his mark on you! We serve a full-time God, Remember that! He's always about you, and you need to always be about Him.

ASK, and it shall be given you; SEEK, and ye shall find; KNOCK, and it shall be opened unto you: for **EVERYONE** that asketh RECEIVETH; and he that seeketh FINDETH; and to him that knocketh it shall be OPENED.

MATT 7:7-8

Know, Love, and Trust
Completely Sold out
Know Him

In business there is a sales philosophy based on know, like, and trust. I think if we applied that similar philosophy of knowing God, loving God, and trusting God we'd be sold out. This is where you truly want to be with your relationship to God. When our relationship is intact we can ask the Father about *near* anything and He will reveal what He wants us to know pertaining to it. God recognizes a sincere heart and will share with us individually on His own accord.

However, there are some things He just doesn't share. One is His Glory, the others you will have to discover for yourself. I have personally received answers to things I prayed about 10 and 15 year ago. (There is no statute of limitations on prayers.) The Messiah once shared *"Ask, and it shall be given you; seek, and ye shall find; knock, and it shall be opened unto you: for everyone that asketh receiveth; and he that seeketh findeth; and to him that knocketh it shall be opened." (Matt 7:7-8)* God is not against us and He's not in the business of withholding things from us for no reason. (Matt 7:11-13)

In certain situations our Father allows us to be assertive. If you have a knowledge and understanding of His nature, countenance, and love you will know when this is practical. Jabez chose such a moment. *"And Jabez called on the God of Israel, saying, oh that thou wouldest bless me indeed, and enlarge my coast, and that thine hand might be with me, and that thou wouldest keep me from evil, that it may not grieve me! And God granted him that which he requested." (1 Chron 4:10* Jabez is only briefly mentioned in this and the previous verse. Without any long discourse, Jabez confidently presents his ambitious petition to the Lord, and the Lord grants him his prayer. What a sensible prayer! The Lord answering his prayer also informs us that they had a relationship. God answers faith; He used this relationship to show His glory.

Love Him

We were made to love and fellowship with God. We all know what it feels like to be loved and to love someone. Can you imagine walking in the Garden with God? God hasn't had that moment again since the separation. God wants our unadulterated love and attention. He's not looking for leftover attention, but if that's all you have left that's a

For I am persuaded
that neither death, nor life, nor angels, nor principalities, nor things present, nor things to come, nor height, nor depth, nor any other creature, shall be able to separate us from the **Love of God,** which is in **Christ Jesus our Lord**
ROMANS 8:38-39

start. We assume that the part-time love we're accustomed to giving is adequate for him. God is love personified, the originator of love, He created that too! (1 John 4:8) His love is boundless. He loves us so much that He gave His son as a ransom offering for our sins, (John 3:16). *"37Nay, in all these things we are more than conquerors through him that loved us. 38For I am persuaded, that neither death, nor life, nor angels, nor principalities, nor powers, nor things present, nor things to come, 39nor height, nor depth, nor any other creature, shall be able to separate us from the love of God, which is in Christ Jesus our Lord." Romans 8:37-39*

I.I.W. (Jer 31:33-34)

33but this shall be the covenant that I will make with the house of Israel; After those days, saith the LORD, I will put my law in their inward parts, and write it in their hearts; and will be their God, and they shall be my people. 34And they shall teach no more every man his neighbour, and every man his brother, saying, Know the LORD: for they shall all know me, from the least of them unto the greatest of them, saith the LORD: for I will forgive their iniquity, and I will remember their sin no more.

Trust Him

The level at which you trust God will be the magnitude in which you see him show up. It's utterly absurd to call on someone you don't trust to help you. Do you trust and believe God has your best interests at heart? If you hesitated you're unsure. Our Father will not abandon you. There are times where it may appear like prayers are falling on deaf ears, but *"The Lord will not leave you, nor forsake you" (Heb 13:5)*. I am convinced that "the teacher doesn't talk during the test". If you're in the midst of a trial trust that He hears your concerns. Since trust is earned, and He has done nothing to break our trust, we should trust Him unwaveringly.

Abba,
You're A
Real
Showoff
And I
Love It..

The Makers Promise
Your Warranty
When a new product is created the maker of the product tests the product through a number of strenuous tasks to test the limits of the product. The product is weighed and measured to assess it's perceived value and effectiveness. After, it's passed all the tests it can be placed into service. Prior to anyone else interacting with the product, the maker issues a warranty that guarantees the product will function according to the design. The warranty also gives instruction to where the product needs to be returned to when it's malfunctioning, along with instructions of how to return the product for repair. God has an infinite warranty. Check your warranty, You are his handy work. Your warranty details will be found in your bible.

Warranties are usually accompanied by user guides and instruction manuals, so the product can be used to its optimal ability. Using a product without ever reading the manuals or guarantees would be considered reckless and dangerous. People around the product could be hurt, injured, or worse. Yet, we see this everyday, everywhere billions of times over.

Misuse
Any modification, change, abuse; accident, tampering, alteration; or unauthorized use of the product, THIS WARRANTY IS VOID. Misuse of a product voids the warranty for 99.99% of manufactures. Except for one. What God creates he backs, guarantees, and repairs. What we see as flaws and defects he sees as an opportunity to show you his glory, what he can do, and how he stands behind his product. When the product left him it was perfect. *"It was good"*. Things along the way are what damage and destroy us, his beautiful product.

Our Father doesn't expect us to stay broken and damaged, but the only way we can be repaired is to get back to the manufacturer. Without going to the Father, you won't get the "fix" you need. All other solutions are duct tape on a bumper. My beloved therapists, physicians, surgeons and medical practitioners are filling in for the original physician. I appreciate all that medical professionals do, but they don't manufacture people for a living. They are substitute repairmen for the original manufacturer.

Check your
Warranty
you're His
Product

Buried Inside Seeds

A seed contains *everything* it needs inside of it. The leaves, the trunk, the roots all lie within the walls of the seed. The seed is merely waiting to be introduced to *good* soil. Not any soil but **good** soil. Within itself it already has all the ingredients for success. Anything that's buried is usually to hide it from thieves. Some people bury precious items. Animals bury food & treats. God buried your seed, your future, inside you where no one else could steal it. All of the valuable things have to be mined and uncovered. Discovering what he buried inside of you is the challenge.

I.I.W. (Job 29:16)

Surely your turning of things upside down shall be esteemed as the potter's clay: for shall the work say of him that made it, He made me not? Or shall the thing framed say of him that framed it, He had no understanding?

Remember Who Created You

The maker of a product declares it's name, what it's functions are and the limitations of the product. The environment the product is in does not dictate the identity or true use of the product. Remember, the maker, dictates the identity of the product, *you*. We are His only creation that has the power to change its environment.

SECTION SUMMARY
Know, Love, and Trust
Get to know God as much as possible.
God wants our love, not our leftovers.
Trust the Lord with your Life.

The Makers Promise - Your Warranty
The maker of a product guarantees the product.
You are His handy work, check your warranty.

Misuse
What God creates He backs, guarantees, and repairs.

Buried Inside Seeds
A seed contains everything it needs inside of it.
God buried your future inside you so no one could steal it.

Remember Who Created You
We are the only creation that can change its environment.

Would you say you know God? Do you trust God? Do you know the gift He buried inside you?

1. Write a list of things you want to change about yourself or your circumstances.
In prayer ask Him what you're suppose
to learn or gain from these things.

Receiving

I.I.W - Luke 6:38
Give, and it shall be given unto you; good measure, pressed down, and shaken together, and running over, shall men give into your bosom. For with the same measure that ye mete withal it shall be measured to you again.

In order to receive what is coming our way it's important to learn *how to* receive. Pride and other countless reasons sometimes make it difficult for blessings and generosity to get to us. The law of sowing and reaping never rests. It's causative nature is finite, meaning it has its limit. Blessing blocking have to be eliminated.

You Didn't Have To

Often times we'll do something for someone and they will reply, "you didn't have to." I often want to reply "No Kidding" but I keep it to myself. The giver in this situation knows they don't have to, they made a conscious decision to do it. It's up to the receiver to receive what has been given to them. Ego and a bunch of other emotional turbulence is interfering with this divine transaction.

Our innate response is self preservation, in this instance our pride or self worth. We never want people to think we need them. It yields power and people may leverage that against us. But in the Kingdom humility is honored. It's ok to accept help from one another but we have to be willing to receive. It's a beautifully balanced circle that feeds itself. Easy givers will in turn become easy receivers.

Example:
One occasion when we were visiting my mother for the weekend we I stayed in a hotel. My mother wanted to give me some money to help with the expenses I had incurred over the weekend. When she tried to give me the money, I bluntly yet playfully replied, *"I'm good, keep it, we got this"*. She retorted sharply; *"Look here, you're gonna take this money or I'm going to hide it somewhere in your bags. God put it on my heart and I know you can use it. Blah, blah, I'm not going to let you block my blessings."* In that moment my pride was stricken, I accepted her gift. The sower is always rewarded for giving, thus you reap what you sow. My mother consciously knew that her seed not being accepted was going to affect her reaping (receiving), and she wasn't having it.

Giving & Receiving

My wife and I try to give frequently, so over time I have grown quite accustomed to receiving gifts randomly; (to include but not limited to the IRS, Old creditors, customers in the form of gratuity, friends, random checks, etc). Every time it's surprising and unique. But I've *grown familiar* with it. As I should, I sow therefore I reap. It's simple and presented in layman's terms. But, after you have sown be willing to receive. No ifs, ands, or buts. It's the kingdoms way.

I.I.W - Pro 11:24 esv
One gives freely, yet grows all the richer; another withholds what he should give, and only suffers want.

How silly would it be to continually ask in prayer, or otherwise, for gifts and favor to just blatantly reject them when their being given to you because you don't recognize what is happening. Praying daily for something and then pushing it away when someone comes to deliver it is ludicrous.

I discovered a long time ago when God revealed it to me in prayer; Anything God does for his children will always involve other people. Even those who shirk their duty as in Jonah's case. Jonah refused his task and God gave him sometime to consider it. Knowing this simple fact gives us the opportunity to be used. What greater pleasure than to participate in the blessing God desires to execute on another.

LEARN TO RECEIVE

STOP REJECTING BLESSINGS AND GIFTS

The Kingdom Doesn't Do Free

King David was at a point of reconciliation and wanted to dedicate a portion of land to God with an altar (2 Samuel 18-25). When David went to consecrate the land and build an altar the land owner offered him free reign of the place and animals for sacrifice. King David would not accept that and offered the owner to buy, "at a price." He wouldn't offer to God that which cost him nothing. Don't offer to God anything that cost you nothing! You need to have some skin in the game. Never diminish the offering you desire to give to God.

Depreciated Value

Free depreciates things. The kingdom pays for everything. Sometimes you're just "paying attention", other times you'll pay monetarily. Paying for something gives it honor. You've already given your time to a task to earn the money. I admit it's enjoyable to receive something for free but over time the things you pay for tend to have greater value to you.

Free services, though helpful for an allotted amount of time, never solve the problem they are trying to eliminate. The quality of free education never measures up to tuition paid schools. Social services, albeit helpful, become a crutch if the individual never adjusts and builds the habits or means to provide the needed income. Across America we see solicitors panhandling for cash everyday taking in an average of $10-$30 per hour and some take in much more.

The local government in Colorado Springs adopted a helpful motto. "Don't give a hand-out, give a hand up" They wanted to encourage people to stop giving the homeless money, but to direct them to the resources that could help them. Because of initiatives like this, one of our local shelter's homeless population declines annually as more of the homeless are helped and re-enter society as productive citizens.

There are working people who get paid far less and struggle to survive, yet still survive. I'm too familiar with the struggle. I've worked three jobs and prayed to just have a single job that would compensate me the same income. I did eventually get that job too! It came with its own share of sacrifices too.

SECTION SUMMARY

You Didn't Have To
It's up to the receiver to receive what has been given to them.
In the Kingdom humility is honored.

Giving & Receiving
After you have sown be willing to receive.
Anything God has for you he gives through others.
Participate in the blessing God desires to give to another.

The Kingdom Doesn't Do Free
Don't offer to God anything that cost you nothing.

Depreciated Value
Free depreciates Things.
The Kingdom pays for everything.

How do you feel when someone gives you something?
Is it awkward for you/them? Why do you feel this way?

....

Find someone to give something to today. You can
start off with something easy like a compliment.
Ex. Flowers, Cup of coffee, Greeting card

MORE
STRAY THOUGHTS
SHORT BUT CHEWY

The Rich Young Ruler   119
Jesus Was Not Poor   120
Staying Humble   121

The Rich Young Ruler
A Missed Opportunity

I.I.W. - (Luke 18:22,23) ESV

[22]"One thing you still lack. Sell all that you have and distribute to the poor, and you will have treasure in heaven; and come, follow me." [23]But when he heard these things, he became very sad, for he was extremely rich.

In my short life I have yet to see generosity not returned when it comes to giving in the Kingdom. I've practiced it countless times solely because of the verse from Malachi 3:10-11. In that verse God asks us to prove Him and see if He won't pour out a blessing. He has stayed true to that promise. I've given as little as $50 and seen it return five and ten fold. God is able and willing to show Himself strong.

When the rich ruler didn't accept the challenge Jesus offered up to him he missed an opportunity for God to show him just how bountiful and righteous the Kingdom can be. Considering just how rich he was it would have took him some time to get rid of all his possessions. The kicker is the minute you start giving, God starts giving. He was so focused on holding onto what he currently had that it clouded his judgment to what was his original question. *"Good Teacher, what must I do to inherit eternal life?" Luke 18:18* He must have really wanted to know otherwise he never would have asked. How often do we do that? We ask a question and then discard the answer because it doesn't line up with what we assumed the answer would be.

I'm going to be gracious because I don't *currently* have that *kind of money*. But I know if I'm in front of the Messiah that I'm going to heed his advice and see what He's trying to demonstrate. Jesus hadn't asked him to lay down his life just to give up his riches and follow him. This rich ruler would've changed history and possibly been counted among the other great disciples. His demonstration of giving would've changed millionaires hearts for centuries to come, *possibly*. We'll never know now because he didn't. What we do know is that he missed a grand opportunity to bless those poor people of that particular city.

Jesus was Not Poor

Being Christlike may mean being more charitable, praying, healing, humility, evangelism, etc. The one trait I never see Jesus displaying is poverty. Let's make one thing clear *JESUS WAS NOT POOR*. For the sake of piety we have "poorer-down" the gospel. The erroneous assumption that our Savior is poor I simply refuse to accept. I'm entitled to my opinion!

❾ Mary, Jesus, and the disciples are at a wedding in Galilee (John 2) and they have no wine. This becomes the first miracle. Prior to this Jesus hadn't performed any miracles. They were coming to Mary and Jesus because they were people of means. You don't ask the poor people at the party to provide beverages! (Some Jewish weddings lasted up to a week or more.) ❽ You have 12 leaders & entrepreneurs stop what they're doing and follow Jesus before he has demonstrated any miracles. Successful men don't keep company with poor people. They surely don't follow poor people. "Birds of a feather, flock together." ❼ Traveling with 12 disciples and himself and he always manages to find a host home that can feed and accommodate 13 additional people.

❻ A group of poor men don't need an accountant (Judas Iscariot). When you find something valuable you want to give or contribute to the cause. It's a safe presumption that people gave or donated, just as we do today. ❺ When a prince is born people bring gifts to pay homage to the prince adding to their wealth. Destitute people were not recipients of gold, frankincense, and myrrh (Matt 2:11). ❹ *"..Though he was rich, yet for your sakes he became poor, that ye through his poverty might be rich." (2 Cor 8:9b)* ❸ Jesus' garments were parted into four pieces and his outer robe, *"coat without seam"*, was auctioned when the guards "caste lots". (John 19:23) That specific robe was rare and valuable, not a pauper's robe. No one auctions worthless clothing.

❷ It is written that there was *"no room for them in the inn"* (Luke 2:6), not that they couldn't afford the inn. They were visiting Jerusalem during the census count. There were just no vacancies. ❶ If Jesus can find a coin in a fish's mouth while he's standing on dry land, it's ok to suggest that he can locate money anytime he needs it. (Matt 17:27)

Staying Humble
Get Grounded

I play a lot of Scrabble, so words are very important to me. When I recently discovered the origin of the word humble I was a little surprised. People use the word all the time but how many people are actually humble. The definition of humble is even more of a disappointment.

(Hum·ble), <u>adjective</u>; [1.] having or showing a modest or low estimate of one's own importance. [2.] of low social, administrative, or political rank. [3.] <u>verb</u>; lower someone in dignity or importance. None of these completely define what it means to be humble, for me. Not to mention I find the definition slightly insulting.

The word humble originates from the word humus (earth or ground), which is also the parent word for human. As a human being we are saying that we are a being formed from the earth. So when you refer to someone as humble, the correct phrasing could be *grounded* or *down to earth*. Hello! To humiliate someone is to bring them back down to earth. Having humility is the act of being humble. Humility is voluntary, while humiliation is forced or out of correction.

The sad definition of humble (above) sounds like someone with self esteem issues when that shouldn't be the case at all. **(Hu·mane), <u>adjective</u>; having or showing compassion or benevolence.** The act of being humble is a beautiful place to be. Your humility allows everyone to see your humanity.

Being humble should be a constant reminder that we came from the earth and this body will in fact return to the earth. The closer you get to the ground the the shorter the fall when you stumble.

I.I.W. - (Pro 16:18)
Pride goes before destruction, a haughty spirit before a fall.

BEWAR
EOFDR
EAMKI
LLERS

THE *Art* OF STORYTELLING

She Called Me Friend	125
Witches Too?	127
To Grow or Not to Grow	129
100 or 500	130
The Praying Lady	132
Bionic Cowboy	134
Tanks But No Thanks	136
No Eggsplanation Needed	138
Walking In The Dark	141
Weeping Prayer	147

When Jesus wasn't casting out demons, healing the sick, forgiving sins, or fellowshipping with the disciples he was telling parables.

I LOVE THE WAY JESUS TELLS A STORY. IT MAKES HIM SO RELATABLE.

Over time, I've identified storytelling as my talking style. I find myself sharing different moments and details about my life in that manner. I wanted this section of the book to be about that. I wanted my granddaughter and family to be able to see what a charmed, blessed life I've been able to live. To God be the Glory!

She Called Me Friend

I.I.W - Matt 25:40
Verily I say unto you, inasmuch as ye have done it unto one of the least of these my brethren, you have done it unto me.

I.I.W - Pro 18:24
A man that has friends must shew himself friendly: and there is a friend that sticketh closer than a brother.

The word friend is a word I hold dear. In our current culture, people use the term friend very loosely. They "friend" you on social media, someone you work with is a "friend". Do you spend quality time with these people? Do they know intimate things about you? Do you know intimate things about them?

One day I received a phone call from a friend and we exchanged the usual pleasantries and then she proceeded to tell me why she was calling. She and her daughter were looking to move into my neighborhood, and they had been looking at homes to rent. While entering the neighborhood her daughter said *"I have a friend that lives over there"*, and Julie replied shockingly, *"I have a friend that lives over there. Which house?" "That house over there."* Julie gave her a concerned look. *"That's where my friend stays! He's a really nice black man."* Julie looked really concerned. *"How do you know Art?" "Oh, I don't know his name but he's my friend.."* Then she commenced to tell her mom how she met me.

One winter morning, while it was snowing, she knocked on my door. I looked through the peephole to see who it was and all I could see was the top of her head. I thought it odd, so I grabbed a mop handle. I just wanted something to defend myself in case it was a home invasion. She was cold and anxious when I opened the door and I kept looking around to make sure no one else was lurking around the corner. When I was confident it was just her I asked her, *"What's up?"* I recall that morning it was bitterly cold, below 20, and slightly windy. She looked cold, scared, and was talking kind of fast. In short, she was stranded and needed help starting her car.

She had knocked on numerous doors and NO ONE, not a one, had answered. I responded *"That really sucks. No problem."* I went into the garage and pulled 150 ft of extension cord and a battery charger into the street and proceeded to jump start her car in the cold. After a few minutes I asked her to try and start the car, and it cranked right up. Up to this point I hadn't paid much attention to the car I was too focused. Start the car, get the girl out of the cold, get back inside where it's warm. Period. When the car started I looked it over, it was a beater. I asked her where she was headed and said a prayer.

She was so happy, she started thanking me and telling me she'd repay me. " No need, glad I could help." I told her to get in, out of the cold, and don't turn off the car for awhile so the battery has time to charge, and turn on the heater.

Well, Julie was calling to thank me for helping her daughter. She was so happy that I helped her. She "Thanked the Universe." Julie was not a believer and didn't really believe in God. But was sincerely thankful that I was willing to help her. I assured her that I help anyone I can, if the role was reversed I'd want someone to help my child.

Point of Reflection

As believers we know and remember a lot of scriptures, but do we walk them out and put them into action. I intentionally try to walk out "this walk". I was a mess when He saved me and I couldn't picture my life without Him. Some things are easy to do and when they present themselves I like to take action.

I.I.W - Matt 22:37-39
Jesus said unto him, Thou shalt love the Lord thy God with all thy heart and with all thy soul, and with all thy mind. This is the first and great commandment. And the second is like unto it, Thou shalt love thy neighbour as thyself.

Witches Too?

I.I.W - Romans 9:15
For he saith to Moses, I will have mercy on whom I will
have mercy, and I will have compassion on whom I will
have compassion. *ref: Exodus 33:19*

I discovered a firebrand named Todd White back in 2015. Todd is an evangelist and pastor of Lifestyle Christianity. When I googled him I found a video of him praying with a young lady who identified as a witch. He walked up to her on the Vegas strip and started ministering to her and she immediately told him she was a witch. He proceeds to talk with her and asked her permission to pray with her. After she agreed he began praying and gets a word of knowledge. He prays for her injury and when he's done she has a bewildered look on her face. Her injury no longer hurts and she's crying and stuttering. He asks her to move around and see how she feels. They converse awhile longer and he reassures her that God loves her.

After watching this witch get healed, I was upset. How could God heal this individual who doesn't believe in him; but here I am with an injury and I've been waiting and believing for healing. My contempt builds up and I get really defiant. *"Oh you're going to heal me too! If she gets healed I'm getting healed."*

So, from that point on I was adamant about being healed. I had bone-on-bone fusion on one knee cap, and an MCL tear. The other knee had an LCL tear. I began speaking immediately about my healing and started doing activities I normally wouldn't. My wife caught me doing some gardening without knee pads one morning and made a suggestion that I go put some on. I told her I didn't need them anymore, my knees were going to be healed, I was fine. So, she left me alone. In two days I planted over 100 sedum in 40 degree drizzling rain in two one hundred feet rows. I stayed outside so long one morning my everything was numb and freezing. I just kept going and mumbling. *"You better hurry up b'cuz I'm not going to quit"*
I honestly don't recall the exact moment I was healed. I carried on that

summer and didn't notice until one day when I ran to the mailbox. I DON'T RUN, at least I didn't back then. I was half way to the mailbox before I realized what I was doing. I grabbed the mail and skipped back to house like a fifth grader. So, the rest of the summer I was test driving my new equipment. During my 5am walks I would sprint from stop sign to stop sign around the neighborhood. What I did realize was that when I was asking for healing, I should have asked for some young lungs. We live in the Rocky Mountains and I hadn't done any physical activity like this since I left Texas. I was panting and gasping for air every time I reached one of those stop signs. Lungs burning but knees just fine!

I.I.W - Genesis 32: 24-26
And Jacob was left alone; and there wrestled a man with him until the breaking of the day. And when he saw that he prevailed not against him, he touched the hollow of his thigh; and the hollow of Jacob's thigh was out of joint, as he wrestled with him. And he said, Let me go, for the day breaketh. And he said, **I will not let thee go, except thou bless me**.

To Grow or Not To Grow

I.I.W - 1 Cor. 10:23
All things are lawful for me, but all things are not expedient:
all things are lawful for me, but all things edify not.

Once, I considered going into the MMJ business since my state, Colorado had recently passed legislation legalizing it. But I was troubled about it. How people may perceive me? Will they question what kind of Christian is he? How will my church feel about those offerings? Will God think wrongly of me? After all, it is a law now. After numerous days of tossing the notion around I went to God in prayer. I personally like to bring God into my major decisions. I need to get better at including Him even in the small decisions. So after two or three days, relatively fast, I received a decisive answer. My father called me. Note, we don't talk daily or even weekly, but when we speak, we speak at length and it's never pointless chatter.

"I'm not sure why God put this on my heart but he wants me to tell you; all things are not sin but, all things are not expedient for you."

"Does that mean anything to you?"

"Yeah, it does.."

If you don't listen what would be the point of asking? Prior to that and many times since then I have seen God use family and friends to relay a message or guidance. Even though it may not always be what I want to hear, I am always elated to hear God answer my questions.

Expedient: a means of attaining an end, especially one that is convenient but could be considered improper or immoral.

Edify: instruct or improve (someone) morally or intellectually.

Point of Reflection
Just because something may not be unlawful or illegal by law does not mean it's something we should involve ourselves with. It may very well be contrary to God's plan for our life. If you're listening or seeking what His plan is for your life.

100 or 500

I.I.W - Luke 6:38
give, and it shall be given unto you; good measure, pressed down, and shaken together, and running over, shall men give into your bosom. For with the same measure that ye mete withal it shall be measured to you again.

I'm a graphic designer by trade but I don't share that with my clients. I prefer sales, fewer headaches. Most people know me as "The Swag Guy" since I supply promo products to businesses. Occasionally, I help out some friends with personal projects. This particular time I was creating graduation invitations, which I created pretty quickly. I sent the art files and invoice for $100 and they paid them shortly after.

As I was cleaning up my desk, my son called, he needed some money for some incidentals. He was in between jobs so he just needed a little money. This happened frequently enough for me to be annoyed but at least he and I had come to terms and he wasn't asking for $1,800. He asked for $70 but I decided if he had $100 then he wouldn't need to ask again for more. I grumbled and pouted a little; I just made $100 and now I'm giving it away. After I sent him the money I went to go transfer the money from the invoice.

The amount they sent was wrong. When I called her she says she didn't make a mistake. She told me they loved my work and they felt I deserved more. I charged her $100 and she paid me $200. As I'm sitting there thinking it over I get convicted. I was sitting there pouting about giving my son money and right then my heavenly Father is doing the same.

God has a very distinct way of teaching me lessons through my children. See our heavenly Father is gracious. I'm sure he wishes we were better stewards but He still takes care of our needs. God made a way to bless me in spite of my poor attitude. That's what Fathers do!

This story doesn't end there… fast forward a few months later and I'm doing my taxes on the weekend. I'm on my work computer doing our taxes and my wife is on her computer ordering nursery furniture for our first granddaughter. I love, love, love the fact that I'm was going to be a "Pop-Pop", but shopping for nursery furniture; hard pass.

As a self-employed business owner I never look to get a refund, I'm content with just keeping my tax liability low. A few hours later I discover we owe just over five hundred dollars. She tells me how much the baby furniture cost, five hundred dollars. What an odd chance. But really, is anything ever a coincidence?

As I'm in the garage smoking a cigar, one of my friends pulls into the driveway. I have a major pet peeve about showing up unannounced. Before I can say anything he's apologizing and shushing me. *"I only stopped b'cuz I saw you standing in the garage so I turned around."* When we get together we tend to be obnoxiously loud. *"I'm headed out of town next week and just wanted to swing by before I left."* I ask him, *"How long you gone for?"* *"Not sure probably a few weeks."* We hug and he turns to leave. He abruptly turns around. *"Oh yeah, this is for you brother!"* He grabs my hand and palms some money to me. I reply, *"What you want me to hold this till you get back?"* *"No, that's for you."* I ask, *"For what? You don't owe me anything."* *"I owe you plenty, but I don't owe you anything. Brother you been good to me and I appreciate you. God, put it on my heart to give this to you."* *"Man, you didn't have to do that!"* Once, again you see how easy it is to forget to receive. *"I'm going to hold it till you get back in case you need it."* This friend sometimes runs short on money but here he was giving me some. But I know how to receive so I shut up and accept it. *"Don't hold on to that money 'cuz of me, I won't be coming back for it."* I respond, *"Not a problem, I know what to do with it."* After he drove off and I looked in my hand it was $500.

Point of Reflection

The dynamic law of sowing and reaping is very specific. *"Do not be deceived, God is not mocked; for whatever a man sows, this he will also reap."* Galatians 6:7 These friend's giving indicated their obedience and desire to create an opportunity for God to do the same for them in the future. God is constantly trying to use each of us to bless each other.

God is never limited to how he wants to deliver a blessing. The kicker is, are we in a position to receive his blessing. If we're bitter, angry, depressed and so on how receptive are we to others needs. In our giving, God wants to make a way for other's to give to us as well. Never assume or estimate how God is going to deliver such blessings.

The Praying Lady

I.I.W - Rom. 13:8
Owe no man anything, but to love one another: for he
that loveth another hath fulfilled the law

On one occasion I was visiting my local Wal-Mart to finalize some sponsorship they had agreed to participate in with one of my community projects. They had been unresponsive to my emails and the store manager was always busy. I totally understood that because I saw him all the time. But I was running out of time and needed to get this project printed. So I go to Walmart like a man-on-a-mission. I head straight for customer service and avoid all the normal pleasantries that always distract me. I'm a talker so it's easy for me to get distracted. *"Hey ladies, I'm strictly business today. Do me a favor and call Jerrod up here. Tell him Art Pierson is here."*

While waiting for the store manager we start chatting. I ask one of them where she had been since I hadn't seen her in awhile. She went into detail about the injury that had been ailing her. I interrupted and apologized. I jumped right into prayer there at the customer service desk. *"Come on, let's pray about it, not talk about it."*

Her coworker bowed her headed as well and we prayed at the customer service desk. The prayer was straight to the point. I lifted my head, opened my eyes, and turned around and the store manager was coming our way. He and I walked off and I waved back at the ladies. After we concluded our conversation I did some shopping of my own and ended up at a register and the lady I prayed with was there. She was really excited so I asked her if she got healed. *"No, I didn't get healed. But the lady behind you saw you praying for me and said she hadn't seen anyone do that in awhile"* "There wasn't anyone behind me." "Yes, there was, an older white lady". "Ok, what happened then?" *Since you prayed for me she wanted to pray for me as well. So I let her pray for me".*

I finished paying and left the store dumbfounded. I was pretty sure there wasn't anyone behind me. If there was someone I have no idea how I missed her. All I did was turn around after praying. Maybe she was angelic, that would be pretty cool too. The end result, someone's healing, matters far more than who prayed. Prayer is a personal thing for most of us but it's also important to pray for one another. I value the opportunity to pray with people, it's one of the easier ways to participate in the Kingdom.

Point of Reflection

The Book says "Love thy neighbor as thyself." If I was hurting and someone knew they could help me I'd hope and pray they would make the attempt and not be concerned with "being embarrassed". It seems that someone is always watching. Make sure you're doing the right thing, if you're going to do anything at all.

After seeing a number of Todd White videos I was amazed at the ease and comfort level he had praying in public everywhere. So I made it a point to pray for others whenever the opportunity arose. Please understand, if you ask God for certain things he will make those opportunities and they're not always easy or comfortable but they will be enlightening and fulfilling.

I.I.W - James 5:16
Confess your faults one to another, and pray one for another, that ye may be healed. The effectual fervent prayer of a righteous man availeth much

Bionic Cowboy

I.I.W - Dan. 4:3 KJV
How great are his signs! And how mighty are his wonders!
His kingdom is an everlasting kingdom, and his dominion is
from generation to generation.

I met David while I was leaving the Wal-Mart. Yep, this is another Wal-Mart story. Those angels and God seem to hang there a lot. Well, David was a greeter, and like most greeters he was well beyond the age of retirement. David had been injured working in another department of the store but didn't want to sit home on worker's compensation but asked to work wherever he could. David wasn't your ordinary Walmart employee though. He was a disabled veteran twice retired. He worked there to supplement his income and get him out the house, and his home was big. He owned a few hundred acres of land. So he had plenty to do.

David was a surly, strong, stubborn no nonsense kinda cowboy. He and I always found common ground on our military service and love of BBQ. We'd get lost in conversation at the front door talking about smoking meat and swapping tips. Great conversations considering his fellow employees said *"He don't talk much"*, so you can imagine my surprise. He seemed to talk to me just fine.

This time in particular I saw him and he was wearing a sling because he had just had surgery. I knew him to be a tough man but surgery on anyone in his 70's is pretty serious. I stopped, asked about his wife.

Have you ever noticed when you ask people how they are, if the response is negative you generally get a long painful explanation. If it's a positive response it tends to be short and brief. Ex. How you doing? Good, Fine!

Not wanting to digest a bunch of negativity, when he paused, I asked him if I could pray with him. David said, *"I don't believe in all of that stuff, I believe in Science."* My reply was, *"Good, God created science, he's in charge of that too."* I bowed my head and begin praying and I could feel David staring at me while my eyes were closed. With all the bad stuff that had been happening to him and his family lately I could understand how he might be a little doubtful of my prayer meaning anything. That didn't change my mind though. David had already had surgery so I couldn't ask for him to be healed but I could desire that he have a speedy and effortless recovery. So I prayed and walked out of the store.

Weeks later a friend and his wife were over visiting and we were talking on my porch. He told me that David had shared with him about his speedy recovery. David told Mark to thank me the next time we spoke. *"You're friend Art has one heck of a line to the man upstairs"* I laughed and asked him what happened.

On one of David's routine physical therapy appointments the doctor was startled after he greeted David. The doctor decided they needed to conduct some strength tests. After all the tests were completed the doctor told David he would need to be extremely cautious. A young man has an average grip strength between 100 psi - 140 psi. A man David's age should be 53 psi - 90 psi. Davids one hand was registering over 1200 psi. The doctor said when he and David shook, he thought David was trying to crush his hand!

Point of Reflection

God doesn't need us to argue and prove his existence, He's capable of showing up on his own behalf. I'm amazed at the manner, the frequency, and way God continues to meet people, me included, where we are. God once again proving that he is a relational and caring Father. People are looking for God to do miracles, but God is waiting for us to step up and serve one another. He wants us to work together in all things.

Tanks, But No Thanks

Back in high school my friend and I intended on going to Black Hills State University in Spearfish, South Dakota. For a South Texas kid South Dakota was worlds away. My buddy John was an A–B student and I was a slacker content with B's. We both applied and the slacker gets accepted and the honor roll student gets rejected. I never told John I was accepted and decided to go to the Army instead.

I scored very well on my enlistment test (86/99). Saying 17 year old Art was naive is an understatement. I may have been bright but I lacked wisdom. The Army offered me all sorts of jobs (I mean a lot), but the moment the recruiter offered me a $10k signing bonus and the GI Bill College Fund I folded like crumpled paper. Currently they offer that to more than half the recruits (the irony). That little signing bonus made me feel like I could buy just about anything. At the time I had my heart set on an Acura Integra. I had no idea how hard they were going to work me for that money.

As the youngest recruit in my armor crewman cycle, I really felt it wasn't that bad. The physical challenge was what you'd expect. Those drill sergeants found muscles I didn't even know existed on my body. I have never been in that physical condition again. The mental conditioning is what tripped up most of the recruits. Many of the recruits weren't accustomed to being treated the way instructors handle you, but I had dealt with far worse before.

TO THIS DAY I HAVE NEVER EXPERIENCED A RUSH LIKE FIRING A TANK

Around week 10 we started working with the tanks hands on. The large majority of our training emphasized personal safety. Our days were filled with cautionary tales as they prepared us for live fire exercises. We were going to experience first hand what an M1A2 Abrams was capable of.

On live fire day everyone was pumped, *I mean everyone!* They feed us like kings and gave us our safety briefing. That morning they shared with us that we were going to use live rounds left over from Desert Storm. Considering most soldiers don't get the opportunity to use live ordinance outside of wartime, it was a big deal. Our biggest concern that morning was range safety and don't aim at wildlife. They couldn't stress the wildlife part enough. Somehow, they knew we were just itching to blow something up.

30 minutes on the range and I needed to go to the latrine. The instructor let me off the tank. When I returned to the firing line, I went to mount the right side of the tank. Just as I was climbing up the tank fired and it threw me 8 ft away onto my back. With my ears ringing and the wind knocked out of me, I was seriously dazed. In that instance an inaudible voice, in my head, screams at me. "HEY! Roll over." "Roll over NOW." With all the strength I could muster I roll over onto my knees on all fours. A fraction of a second later the tank fires again. I look over my right shoulder and see the tank barely glide past me and settle back into place.

I'm dumbfounded, stuck, and scared senseless. Did I almost get run over by a tank? As I get to my feet I lock eyes with the instructor on the tank next to us. The look on his face is priceless. Big eyes, pale as a ghost with his mouth hanging open. I signal for him to call my tank and put my finger to my mouth (shhhh). A near miss accident like that would have all of us in trouble. Me, the instructors, and so on.

From that moment forth all I could imagine was how was I going to navigate another 44 months in one of these tanks. Things worked out so smoothly over the next 3 years that I only spent my last 8 months of service on a tank. God knew me and he knew that I wasn't cut out for that. I completed my enlistment and the rest is history. Tanks, but No Thanks!

Point of Reflection

I learned a multitude of things from this event. Anytime someone gives you an incentive you should be aware of what it is they're asking of you. No one just gives away $10k. Nothing is free and if they say it is run, run fast. The job that everyone wants doesn't need you to give away anything to attract people to it. None of the low risk high retention jobs offer incentive bonuses.

Angels are real and I've made the ones assigned to protect me work to hard. *Psalms 91:11-12* *[11]For he shall give his angels charge over thee, To keep thee in all thy ways. [12]They shall bear thee up in their hands, Lest thou dash thy foot against a stone.* God has been very patient with me throughout my life and spared me from myself and others. This just happens to be an example of him rescuing me once again. God is good, ALLthe time!

No Eggsplanation Needed

I.I.W - Job. 5:9 KJV
He performs wonders that cannot be fathomed,
miracles that cannot be counted.

One morning while posting something on social media, I saw a picture of eggs for 55¢. At first I thought it was a throwback Thursday post and didn't pay it too much attention. Soon after I left to run errands at my local grocery store and discovered it was current. I asked the stocker why the eggs were so cheap. *"What's wrong with them?"* He said that they had ordered too many and that they needed to move them or they would have to trash them all when they expired. Remember, I'm a talker so next thing you know he's showing me the stacks and stacks of eggs in the cooler.

There were thousands of eggs! All I could think about was how many they were going to throw away. I bought seven or so dozen so I could help out but still left feeling a little discouraged. I returned home and dropped off my groceries, then decided to make a few office visits with the eggs. In all honesty, I was wanting to drum up some business and show a little generosity at the same time. My first stop was my local dentist office. I greeted the ladies in the front office as usual.

They immediately started laughing and asked if I got lost leaving the grocery store! I told them about the store having too many eggs. Since I was giving them eggs they didn't need to shop for eggs. They could treat themselves to a coffee instead since I had just saved them the money. The ladies smiled, took the eggs, and I was out the door. Then I stopped at the bank adjacent to the dentists and did the same.

Later that evening, I was sharing with my wife how my day went and how I went and gave out eggs that morning. *"They probably think your husband is some weirdo going around handing out eggs. But everyone I offered them to did take them."* She asked if I knew anywhere that I could take A LOT of eggs. She suggested a local food pantry and I commented that that pantry doesn't see enough people to move that many eggs. Then, I thought about a local shelter downtown. They house and feed hundreds of homeless daily. *"It's got to be a burden to feed hundreds of people three meals daily!"* we both said simultaneously. *"Springs Rescue Mission."* Later that evening I called a friend to ask if he wanted to tag-along. He laughed and said he was going down there tomorrow to see about volunteering. Perfect, we can ride together and Aaron, my son would ride with us.

The next morning I went egg shopping and bought 110 dozen. Come on, at 55¢ it wouldn't even put a dent in the bank. When we arrived at the rescue mission we had to find where to take these eggs. Back then the mission was already half a city block. One of the volunteers told me I was in the wrong building and pointed us in the right direction. My friend Andre reminded me that he needed to find the director to talk with him. No exaggeration, as soon as we walked in we were greeter by a man in a hard hat, he was the director of the mission! I told him what I was doing and he went and found the head chef and instructed me to drive around the back. When the chef came out side I explained once again emphasizing that I had in fact paid for these. A man pulling eggs out of the trunk of his car may seem a little shady to some.

The chef stood quietly still for a few moments. When he finally spoke, voice cracking he asked me if he could hug me! Said he was a hugger. I hesitated for a moment then replied *"I'm a hugger too!"* He motioned for me to come see something. As they opened up the large walk-in refrigerator, he pointed to a large empty shelf. There was a completely empty shelf with one single cracked egg dripping.

We both looked at each other in astonishment. He proceeds to tell me that he was praying the night before. He didn't get his shipment of eggs and was wondering what he was going to prepare for the people the next day. Well, his prayer was answered. I stood there tongue tied and trying to speak while I was choking on the words. Anyone who knows me, knows I'm never at a loss for words. I managed to squeak out a response, *"What if I hadn't listened."* He immediately replied, *"But you did, you did listen."* I was here on a whim, at least I thought so. I just wanted to get those eggs out the store and help a few more people in the process. The harsh reality is that those thirteen hundred eggs only

THE WORLD IS WAITING ON OUR OBEDIENCE

cover about two meals. Andre, Aaron and I looked at each other dumbfounded. They patted me on the shoulder and we drove away.

Once again that evening I shared how my day went with my wife and we agreed that I should do the same for the local food pantry she had mentioned the day before. So the next morning I went and purchased another hundred dozen eggs. I dropped them off at the food pantry and all those eggs were distributed that very day as well. Never again have I seen the store do another goof up like that. That week I spent a little more than $115 and managed to get more than two hundred and ten dozen eggs to strangers. I'm sincerely happy that I was able to help the store and all those people. Other than a little gas, it really didn't cost us much. God is so good!

Point of Reflection

God hears all of our prayers. What I surmised from this experience is that he's always looking to work through all of us. If He can just get your attention you can be used. He continually uses those who make themselves available to be His hands. What I assumed was trivial was of the utmost importance to the other believer waiting for an answer to his prayer. How many other people were used in situations in my life when I called upon the Lord to assist me in my times of need. That moment made me aware of how significant all of our actions really are in the larger scheme of things. Glory be to God, the most high!

I.I.W - Dan. 4:3 KJV
How great are his signs! And how mighty are his wonders!
His kingdom is an everlasting kingdom, and his dominion
is from generation to generation.

Walking In The Dark
The Mid Term

I.I.W - Deut. 31:6 KJV
Be strong and courageous. Do not fear or be in dread of them, for it is the Lord your God who goes with you. He will not leave you or forsake you."

In the early morning hours I enjoy walking with God's word playing in my ear. It's so peaceful and I find that I absorb more of the word with limited distractions. This one morning I was distracted. My wife and I had been at odds about our current home. She was tired of our current neighborhood and I was happy with my home, it was a nice home. I felt if we moved I wanted to be in a wooded area with lots of trees, but she wanted a home that had a view. We live in the Front Range of the Rocky Mountains, so there's no shortage of views. I assumed that either of those solutions was going to cost us more than we could currently afford.

As I'm walking in the dark that morning, I ask the Father if there was a solution to this, reveal it to me. She wants a view of the mountains and I'd like some tress, lots of them; seeing some wildlife would be great. I finish my morning walk and start my day as normal.

A few days pass and I'm at a local Chamber of Commerce meeting. I shake hands and greet members as usual but nothing special. After the meeting Dave and I exchange pleasantries and start chatting about the real estate market and I inquire about what's out there. I mention to him that I'm not in the market to buy a new house but I was curious what 5 to 10 acres would cost. I ask him to run a query and send me some stuff to "just peek" at. I remind him that I'm not a serious buyer so don't spend too much time on it. He nods and says he'll look into it.

Mr. Dave specializes in rural and ranch properties. My friend Dave reminds me of Sam Elliot. Dave is rugged and cool with no nonsense. I'm a believer that God places the right people in your path for the right moments. This became evidently clear in dealing with Dave.

At the time I had over a dozen real estate clients but none of them handled country homes like Dave, at least not to my knowledge. A day later Dave sent me an email and I share it with my wife while we watch homes on TV. Looking at the listings between commercials, I like a few of the houses but nothing really grabbed our attention, not to mention all the homes were between 300k to 800k. We bought our current home at 150k. So I was feeling a little overwhelmed.

Just as we close the laptop we see two more listings that had been recently posted. One was one day old and the other 20 days old. Since houses were selling like hot cakes the 20 days on market was kind of an alarm. The listing photos for that home looked great, the photos of the other, not so great and it was a log cabin. Ewww, I didn't want to live in a log cabin home. I look at the photos anyway, nothing too impressive. So I email Mr. Dave and ask him to schedule home showings on these two.

That Thursday was pretty normal until about 2 hours before the showing. Scattered showers on a Rocky Mountain summer are fairly normal. This day in particular, the weather was turning horrible. There were tornado warnings, flash flood warnings, and some small hail was bouncing around outside at that moment. 45 minutes before our appointment, I call Dave to ask him what it looks like at his home. He tells me its pouring down and his driveway is washed out and covered with water. He asks if I want to reschedule. *"No let's stick to the plan and I'll check back with you."* He hangs up but doesn't sound too sure it's going to happen.

After I get off the phone, I begin praying earnestly in the kitchen. I had seen Chip Brim speak once and he shared a story about rebuking a tornado in his neighborhood in Oklahoma. His house and his neighbors houses were the only homes not damaged during that storm, not a shingle out of place. I remember telling myself *"You gotta dig in Art, the kingdom suffers violence and the violent take by force."*

I'm walking around the living room praying loud and causing just as much ruckus as the storm outside. *(Years later, I now know the volume of your voice doesn't change anything about the prayer.)* Ten minutes later the storm stops! The sun literally shines like it hadn't rained all day. Later I learn that there was a tornado that touched down and ran through Falcon Storage less than four miles away. *(Google: Falcon storage tornado).*

I call back Mr. Dave and let him know I'll meet him at the first home in 30 minutes. This also allowed me to see how the two homes handle a real downpour. We arrive at the first home; the photos were great, the home fell short. We leave and literally go around the block to the other home about 12 acres away. This home is the exact opposite. This home is remodeled on the inside but has poor photos and is ugly on the outside because of five foot tall grass all over the property. My wife says that they should cut the grass.

"No, they shouldn't, then more people will come look at it." "This isn't anything a riding mower can't change." I'm a graphic designer so I can see the beauty through the mess. Inside everything is perfectly ok. We walk throughout the house a couple times mentally putting furniture in rooms. As we walk outside we stare at each other. We both say *"I like it."*

Dave asks if we want to make an offer. First understand that my wife and I never agree upon the same thing this easily. We look at each other and agree, *"Yeah, we want it, make an offer."* Remember, we weren't even looking to buy, at least that's what we thought. Dave asks about a qualification letter. We don't have one. So, we put an offer in without being qualified. (I know all the real estate agents reading this will cringe at that.) We arrange for Dave to come see our home two days later on Saturday.

When Dave arrives he asks if we just cleaned up before he came; he comments, *"It looks like a model home."* You don't have to get ready when you stay ready! I'm a steward, I like to take care of everything God entrusts to me. We had been waiting for a moment like this. This house had been waiting for an opportunity like this. I do my best to treat everything God gives me as if it were on loan.

We complete the loan application over the weekend and schedule for photos to be taken on Monday, two days later. As he's preparing

I TAKE CARE OF EVERYTHING GOD ENTRUSTS TO ME

for the photographer he asks about the letter. *"We don't have it yet, it just went in today."* He gives a concerned look. *"Well there's another offer, you gotta get it to me soon."* They took their photos and as they wrap up he asks me about the letter again. *"Dave, are you a praying man?" "Well I guess so." "Well I'm going to let you know you'll never see a transaction like this one again." "Ok!"*

After they leave, my wife comes home for lunch and I share with her the urgency of getting qualified. (My wife previously worked for this financial institution.) She calls the loan officer directly. The loan officer **THREE HOURS LATER** tells her that most applications are backed up 2 to 3 weeks, but she can try and get to it as soon as 2-3 days. That wasn't the answer I was hoping for. So, my wife and I pray on the front porch. Three hours later I receive an email from the loan officer, it's the letter! That gives me just enough time to get it over to my Realtor. The selling agent is wrapping up for the day and is irritated by the late offer.

We supply him with the mortgage officer's personal contact. (She told us to. ☺) The seller's agent claims he can't get in touch with her. We call her, she answers. We go back and forth with this issue for awhile. I let Dave know we're going to be unavailable the rest of the week, we're headed to an event out of town. The next morning we head to a Healing Conference up in Woodland Park, CO.

Throughout the morning Dave and I text back and forth. Around 9am, Dave lets me know that the seller has accepted the other offer! I'm stunned, the other offer was less with contingencies. I offered full asking price with no contingencies. **Why!** He asks me what I want to do. I'm stuck, I feel defeated. I've seen God move on our behalf so many times. My Lord has **NEVER** failed me. I sit speechless and wait to share this with my wife. We had taken off a week from work to be at this event and I wanted her to focus on the conference. So I text Dave, *"Go grab a cup of coffee and watch what my God does."* I won't lie, I get a *little cocky* when it comes to my Father. I've witnessed him do so many beautiful and unusual things. Dave responds back, *"Ok"*. Awkward silence for a few hours.

During the lunch break I share the fallout with my wife. Kimberly keeps asking me questions but all the answers I have speak against the outcome I'm believing for. I try to stay positive but I'm confused and unnerved. Kimberly keeps asking me about other options. I tell her. *"I want that house for us."* As we're entering a restaurant I'm about to finally answer her question. Just before I open my mouth, the phone rings. It's Dave, and he's excited. *"I've never seen this before Art, they pulled the offer, What do you want to do?"* *"Dave, give them what they want!"* Of course now, they accept our offer!

Afterwards, the problems still don't let up. The seller doesn't want to pay for a well inspection. We pray about it and decide we'll proceed. Then after inspection the seller doesn't want to give us $2,800 for needed repairs. My wife tells Dave to proceed and we agree on $1,500 and then Mr. Dave decides to give us money. This is one of those moments where God places someone in the right position. Dave felt what we were asking was fair. Everyone needs a Dave in their life.

Homes in our area were flying off the market. The average days on market was two and a half to four and a half days, ours stayed on the market for 19 days. In those 19+ days I wondered what was wrong with our home. Our home had just been painted the previous month. None of the listing reviews had any complaints or suggestions. I work from home so every time there was a showing I had to vacate. I was aggravated and tired of leaving my home well before the 24th showing.

Once again, we pray that the right family with the right offer would get the home. Two days later we received two offers, one over one under. We accept the first offer! When that house finally sold we became the highest comp in the neighborhood at the time!

The home we purchased fulfilled all the things I asked for in prayer! The south side of the property has a view of the Pikes Peak mountain range, the east faces the Eastern plains; you can see 15 miles away. The North side faces a forest. Our yard is covered in well over 100 trees. The way the home sits, the trees don't obstruct any of the views. Quite frequently we have groups of deer visiting. I've counted over 15 at a time. It's an equestrian community so several of my neighbors have horses. It's far more satisfying watching horses than pedestrians. The neighbors refer to our property as the fortress since it has such a large concentration of trees in comparison to their properties. Surely God is always faithful.

Point of Reflection

"You have not because you ask not, or you ask amiss." That is a huge understatement. The entire time from from walking in the morning to moving into the new home was less than 50 days. That's extremely fast. God managed to work all those elements out and coordinate people, moving timelines, an example of favor upon favor. In those 50 days the new home had appreciated 30K!

I referred to this story as The Midterm because with all that I experienced in the test and learned, it only expanded my understanding and belief in what God can and will do. As you get stretched he shows you more and more each time. This test was the first of many others.

In Ron Carpenter's book: *The Necessity of an Enemy* he mentions, "The Teacher never talks during the Test." That is true, it can be quite lonely and overwhelming while you're waiting for the test results. If we simply understood just how much The Father loves to spoil and provide for his children we wouldn't worry. Not because He's giving us something but because He's a good father.

Say exactly what you want and stick with it. Understand the reason for being impeccable with your word. When you have the King's attention make sure you use the time correctly and be detailed.

I.I.W - 2 Chron 16:9a AMP
For the eyes of the LORD move to and fro throughout the earth so that he may support those whose heart is completely His.

I.I.W - 1 Thes 5:7
Pray without Ceasing.

Weeping Prayer

I.I.W - 2 King 6:17 KJV
And Elisha prayed, "Open his eyes, Lord, so that he may see." Then the Lord opened the servant's eyes, and he looked and saw the hills full of horses and chariots of fire all around Elisha.

There are some things you just shouldn't pray for. I know that sounds odd but there are some things you're better off not getting unless you're truly ready. Some people are praying for a million dollars but they have a thousand dollar mentality. You're not ready for a million yet. That money will break you, I mean BREAK YOU! You'd spend the first 750k shopping and the last 250k in counseling. God is not trying to do that or put you through that. I've prayed for patience in the past, that's another ill-prepared prayer. Anyone that's ever asked for patience knows exactly what I mean.

As a habit I make prayer lists like people make New Year's resolutions. It's my weird way of saying "Let me see what God is going to do this time." Over time I've learned three solid things. One: God has a sense of **humor**. His humor is not always ha ha funny, but Boom!, I got ya! Two: God is all about the theatrics, the **drama**. The Father likes to make a statement when he shows up. Third: no matter what he **loves** you. He doesn't care if you're atheist, Christian, purple, or arrogant. Knowing these things about him, I like to see him *do things*. I don't <u>need</u> to see him do things, I enjoy watching him work. God is full of surprises, He doesn't disappoint.

I once asked God to show me what he feels, for Him to show me what matters to Him. At first it felt like a great idea. Let me be honest, that's a horrible prayer. God handles that for us. We're not designed to take in all that pain and sorrow. After that prayer my awareness of people's pain was like a beacon. For days I found myself looking at just about every injured person in public, or staring in certain directions too long. It was like these people were waving their hand and saying *"look over here I'm hurt, I'm depressed, I'm angry."* After the second or third day I was totally over it.

I went grocery shopping and of course He was pointing the people out. So every time I saw a person I would mumble *"Bless them Lord, Bless them."* As I go into the canned goods section I have this overwhelming urge to cry. But it's been years since I had that feeling with this force. I'm whispering *"Not now, don't do that here, not here in the grocery store."* I realize that the feeling isn't going away so I turn and try to walk faster, before I realize it I'm running to the exit. Crying at church is one thing, bawling in the grocery store, that's a completely different thing. As I exit the store I'm praying out loud. *"Thank you for not embarrassing me father. I get the point"* Then I begin professing how I shouldn't have asked that of him.

▲ The Holy Spirit Shows up How It Wants To ▲

❶ The first time the Holy Spirit came upon me I was volunteering at a youth conference in Houston. It began during praise & worship. Almost everyone in attendance wept for over an hour. ❷ **One time the Holy Spirit visited me, and it healed me in my garage while a friend prayed over the phone. I paced around the house like an addict for 3 hrs, and God answered old questions I had asked.** ❸ Another time the Holy Spirit visited me at a Men's Advance up at Charis Bible College. Andrew Wommack led us in prayer and three minutes later over 100 of us were speaking in tongues. The sound in the room felt like a roaring football stadium. My friend beside me said he couldn't hear a thing, just me and the other men. Each time the spirit came in a different way and manner. Sometimes I get goosebumps when I'm speaking about God.

Point of Reflection

This experience revealed to me that God has a lot of hurt children and that there are plenty of people to pray for, believers and non-believers. There is no shortage of the hurt and broken. There were people that looked physically normal but I could feel the pain and anger they were carrying. We truly never know what people are going through which is why it's a good habit to not be so reactive when people lash out. That need to give unsolicited advice should also be restrained. "Walking in someones shoes" is one thing you don't want to do. I truly feel I needed that experience. It made me a more compassionate person.

Authors Favorite Reading List

The Power of Positive Thinking, *Norman Vincent Peale*

The Authority of the Believer, *John A. MacMillan*

Business Secrets from the Bible, *(Rabbi) Daniel Lapin*

Thou Shalt Prosper, *Rabbi Daniel Lapin*

The Laws of Thinking, *E. Bernard Jordan*

Cosmic Economics, *E. Bernard Jordan*

As a Man Thinketh, *James Allen*

The 7 Habits of Highly Effective People, *Stephen R. Covey*

The Necessity of an Enemy, *Ron Carpenter Jr.*

Think and Grow Rich, *Napoleon Hill*

How to Win Friends & Influence People, *Dale Carnegie*

Psycho-Cybernetics, *Maxwell Maltz*

The Principle and Power of Kingdom Citizenship, *Myles Munroe*

The Power of Your Subconscious Mind, *Joseph Murphy*

The ABCs of Success, *Bob Proctor*

The Dynamic Laws of Prosperity, *Catherine Ponder*

The Four Agreements, *Don Miguel Ruiz*

You^2, *Price Pritchett*

The Secret Kingdom, *Pat Robertson*

The Richest Man in Babylon, *George S. Clason*

The QBQ: Question Behind the Question, *John G. Miller*

The Miracle Power of the Mind, *Joseph Murphy*

Think, Learn, Succeed *By Dr. Caroline Leaf*

The Science of Changing Your Mind, *Joe Dispenza*

Dear Esteemed Supporters,

If Beware of Dream Killers has touched your heart and ignited a spark, I humbly ask for your support. Together, let's nurture the belief that God's plan for us is boundless.

Our beliefs about God and ourselves shape the fabric of our lives, yet doubt can hide even the simplest truths. God's wisdom, often concealed in plain sight, challenges even the sharpest minds. Belief is the key that unlocks our potential, and I firmly believe we can step into the visions He has bestowed upon us.

Your contribution will propel this message of self-discovery, gratitude, and transformation even further. Let's journey onward together, drawing closer to our divine purpose, and becoming the vibrant people we were destined to be.

Your support, whether through donations, using the book in discussion groups, or contributing to future projects, fuels this mission of empowerment. Your generosity is a blessing!
Thank you for walking with us on this journey.

Send Donations to:
Pierson Legacy Publishing
12770 Cherokee Trail Dr.
Elbert, CO 80106

or contact us directly at:
plegpub@gmail.com

With heartfelt gratitude,
Artemus L. Pierson

Hear, O Israel: The Lord our God is one Lord: And thou shalt Love The Lord Thy God wit all thine Heart, with all thy Soul, and With all thy Might. And These Words, Which I command Thee this day, shall be in thine Heart: and thou shalt teach them Diligently unto thy children, and shalt talk of them when thou sittest In thine house, and when thou walkest by the way, & when thou liest down, & when thou risest Up. Duet 6:4-7